3/96

PRESIDENTS
VERSUS
CONGRESS

Conflict and Compromise

OTHER FRANKLIN WATTS BOOKS
BY EDMUND LINDOP

ASSASSINATIONS THAT SHOOK AMERICA
PRESIDENTS BY ACCIDENT
THE BILL OF RIGHTS AND LANDMARK CASES
CUBA
AN ALBUM OF THE FIFTIES
THE TURBULENT THIRTIES
THE DAZZLING TWENTIES
THE FIRST BOOK OF ELECTIONS

PRESIDENTS
VERSUS
CONGRESS

Conflict and Compromise
BY EDMUND LINDOP

Democracy in Action
Franklin Watts
New York   Chicago   London   Toronto   Sydney

Library of Congress Cataloging-in-Publication Data

Lindop, Edmund.
Presidents versus Congress : conflict and compromise / by Edmund
Lindop.
p.   cm. — (Democracy in action)
Includes bibliographical references and indexes.
ISBN 0-531-11165-2
1. Presidents—United States—History—Juvenile literature.
2. United States. Congress—History—Juvenile literature.
3. Separation of powers—United States—History—Juvenile
literature. I. Title. II. Series.
JK585.L56   1994
353.03'13'09—dc20   93-30784 CIP AC

To the James Ostiller family,
with many thanks for your steadfast support,
kindness, humor, and cherished friendship

CONTENTS

PRESIDENTS
VERSUS
CONGRESS

Conflict and Compromise

PROLOGUE

THE FRAGILE EXPERIMENT

The Constitution that the Founding Fathers created in 1787 as the framework of government for the infant republic of the United States was a unique document. Unlike most European countries, which were ruled by kings whose power was nearly unlimited and who claimed that their authority was granted them by God, the United States was conceived as a democracy in which the people ruled through the representatives they elected to serve them.

The powers of the federal government of the United States were divided among three branches—the executive branch, headed by a president; the legislative branch, which was to consist of a bicameral (two houses) Congress made up of the Senate and the House of Representatives; and the judicial branch, which consisted of the federal courts. This federal government was to share its authority to govern with the governments of the states. The federal government could exercise only those powers delegated to it by the Constitution, such as declaring war; all other powers were retained by the states.

Many people living in the late eighteenth century regarded the United States as a fragile experiment. They believed that the Constitution left the federal government, with its division of power among the various branches, too weak to rule and predicted that it was doomed to failure. But the Founding Fathers had good reasons for establishing a government of shared powers. By dividing government power almost equally among the three branches, the Founding Fathers hoped to eliminate the danger that any single individual—such as a king or dictator—could seize power. And if the federal government had not shared power with the states, the Constitution never would have been ratified, or approved. (Nine of the thirteen original states had to approve the Constitution in order for it to become the law of the land.)

This constitutional concept of separation of powers is maintained by a system of "checks and balances." Each branch of the federal government is subject to a number of constitutional checks (restraints) by either or both of the others. For example, Congress has the sole power to make laws, but the president may prevent bills passed by Congress from becoming law by vetoing (rejecting) them. In its turn, Congress can override a presidential veto by a two-thirds vote in each house. The federal courts have the power to decide whether national and state laws are in accord with the Constitution—and to strike down those they find to be unconstitutional. The president has the power to appoint federal judges, cabinet members, and other officers in the executive department, but these appointments must be confirmed, or approved, by the Senate. Congress has the authority to impeach (remove from office for reason of wrongdoing) officeholders in the judicial and executive departments of the government, including Supreme Court justices and other federal judges, the president, and the vice president.

The separation of powers between the president and the Congress also extends to foreign affairs. Under the Constitution, the president is responsible for foreign relations, but only Congress can appropriate whatever funds are required to conduct foreign policy. The president nominates the United States's various ambassadors and ministers to foreign countries, but their appointments are subject to the approval of the Senate. Though only Congress has the power officially to declare war, the president, as commander in chief of all the armed services, determines how the nation's military forces will be employed. The president has the authority to negotiate treaties, but they must be ratified by a two-thirds vote of the Senate.

Separation of powers has inevitably led, at times, to serious clashes among the three branches of the federal government. This book examines some of the most important conflicts that have occurred between the executive and the legislative branches.

Such conflicts between the president and Congress are as old as the nation itself and continue to take place. This is one reason why each new presidential administration, such as that of Bill Clinton, places such a great emphasis on establishing solid relations with Congress. Without such relations, a president, despite the power granted him by the Constitution, can find it very difficult to get his government programs enacted.

Friction between the president and Congress has usually been most intense when the chief executive belongs to one political party and Congress is controlled by the leading opposition party. Since the Civil War, the Democrats and the Republicans have been the two major political parties in the United States. Since 1955, Republican presidents have usually been faced with a Congress in which the Democrats controlled one, and often both, of the houses. For nearly forty years, this "divided government" made it difficult for Republican presidents to achieve their legislative goals. At the same time, Congress found it difficult to enact legislation, since many of the bills it passed were vetoed by the president. It is important to remember, however, that such a situation rarely results in complete governmental paralysis. The popularity of a president with the electorate, for example, may be enough to convince members of the opposition party in Congress to cooperate with the president's legislative program. Members of opposing parties also may find reason to compromise, often because of overlapping mutual interests, and the business of government does continue.

Divisions along party lines are not the only cause of deadlocks between the executive and legislative branches of the federal government. Often there are opposing factions, or groups, within the same political party. For example, southern Democrats in Congress blocked civil rights measures that were proposed by Democratic Presidents Harry Truman and John F. Kennedy. These Democrats from the South tended to be more conservative than most other members of their party, and they often voted with Republicans on economic issues. Because the views they expressed were shared by a majority of voters in the states or congressional districts they represented, these legislators were not fearful that opposing a Democratic president would cost them their seats in Congress.

Such conflicts between the executive and the legislative branch lead to a government that can seem inefficient and wasteful. Wouldn't it be better, frustrated citizens often argue, when an important piece of legislation is stalled by political fighting between the president and Congress, if the president could just do what he wanted? Why should the president have the right to veto legislation that both houses of Congress have passed? In a dictatorship, it is true, results are sometimes achieved more quickly, without the endless political haggling that seems to accompany each piece of government business in this country. Because the citizens of the United States have chosen to keep the powers of government separate, we have intentionally sacrificed some of the ease and efficiency that dictators enjoy in carrying out their policies. But we have gained something far more precious—freedom from tyranny and the priceless treasure of liberty.

This book will discuss fifteen important conflicts between presidents and Congress, ranging in time from George Washington's administration through George Bush's presidential term, involving both foreign and domestic affairs. The specific issues involved include the conduct of wars and the ratification of treaties, civil rights legislation, a possible constitutional amendment, the impeachment of a president, the Senate's contested confirmation of a presidential appointment, the Watergate scandal, and the Iran-contra affair. While this treatment is in no way exhaustive—every administration has, at one time or another in its term in Washington, found itself at odds with Congress—the reader will find here an introduction to some of the most important, and interesting, constitutional clashes between the legislative and executive branches.

GEORGE WASHINGTON

JAY'S TREATY

Article II, section II, of the Constitution states that the president "shall have power, by and with the advice and consent of the Senate, to make treaties." When George Washington became the nation's first president in 1789, he assumed that the Senate would work closely with him regarding treaties. Washington believed that in this regard the Senate would be quite similar to the council, or upper house, of the colonial legislatures, whose members had been appointed either by the British king or by the royal governor in eleven of the thirteen colonies. One of the council's chief functions had been to advise the governor on important policies.

In August 1789, Washington paid the Senate a visit to seek advice on a treaty he intended to make with the Creek Indians. After laying the proposed treaty before the senators, the president read them several questions about it and waited for their replies. A long, uneasy silence followed, broken only when one of the senators, implying that the legislators would like privacy in which to confer on the treaty, moved that the document be referred to a committee. His colleagues agreed that this was the correct procedure, infuriating Washington, who had expected that the senators would work cooperatively with him as a team. "This defeats every purpose of my coming here," he angrily declared, and strode out of the chamber.[1]

The Senate thus served notice on Washington that its constitutional responsibilities did not include giving the president informal advice. Instead, the legislators were determined to exert complete independence in discussing proposals and making decisions. This early encounter between the chief executive and one house of Congress demonstrates that from the beginning of the American republic each branch of the government zealously guarded its own powers.

A few years later, the United States faced its first grave international crisis. By 1794, U.S. relations with Great Britain had deteriorated to the point that war seemed imminent. The most aggravating American grievance was Britain's insistence on maintaining forts and trading posts in the Old Northwest (the region north of the Ohio River and east of the Mississippi River). By the terms of the Treaty of Paris, which had ended the Revolutionary War in 1783, the British had promised to hand over these forts and posts to the Americans. Instead, they kept these outposts in order to reap rich profits from the fur trade and hold back American expansion into the area. American frontiersmen were especially outraged by the British practice of arming the Indians of the Old Northwest and encouraging them in their hostility toward the pioneers.

There were also other reasons for strife between Great Britain and the United States. The British at this time were at war with France, and they took various steps to prevent the United States from trading with France and its colonies. Needing seamen for their navy, they boarded American ships and impressed (kidnapped) sailors. In the British West Indies, which were dependent on American trade for provisions, the British seized many U.S. ships and threw their crews into miserable dungeons. At one time there were more than two hundred American merchant vessels held in British ports in the Caribbean Sea.

The political party system in the United States was just beginning in the 1790s, and the two new parties were in large part defined by their differing attitudes toward the Anglo-French conflict. Most Republicans (also called Democratic-Republicans) were strongly pro-French.* Led by Thomas Jefferson and James Madison, the Republicans praised the French for helping the American cause in the Revolutionary War and cheered them for overthrowing their king and establishing a republic in 1792. The Republicans were opposed by the Federalist party, headed by Alexander Hamilton and John Adams. The Federalists generally were pro-British, primarily because Britain—in spite of its antagonistic policies toward the United States—was the new republic's most important trading partner. The Federalists knew that war with Britain could prove disastrous to American commerce.

Merchants and shippers tended to support the Federalists, but many other Americans were avid Republicans and openly hostile toward Britain. In New York City, citizens built fortifications against a possible British invasion. An unruly mob in Charleston, South Carolina, tore down a statue of William Pitt, the British statesman who had played a large role in helping Britain and its colonies win the French and Indian War and father of the current prime minister. At Marblehead, Massachusetts, three thousand volunteers, reviving the spirit of the "Minutemen," reached for their rifles and began drilling on the common in preparation for war with Britain.

Even the most ardent Federalists were forced to admit that war with Britain appeared very near. Congress

*This was not the modern Republican party, which began in 1854.

empowered Washington to summon eighty thousand state militia if necessary. Bills were passed authorizing the construction of six frigates as the first vessels for a navy. Despite such preparations, the military forces of the United States were pitifully weak compared with those of Britain. With no standing army or navy the Americans had little chance to wring any concessions from Britain through warfare.

Realizing that war with Great Britain would be extremely damaging to the infant republic, Washington decided that such conflict must be prevented if at all possible. His Federalist supporters concurred. Federalist congressman Fisher Ames solemnly declared, "The line of duty is plain—peace, peace to the last day it can be maintained."[2]

Washington decided to send a special envoy to London to negotiate a treaty with Britain. For this important task he selected John Jay, chief justice of the Supreme Court, and sent his name to the Senate, where his appointment was confirmed by a vote of 18 to 8, with 4 senators abstaining (not casting ballots).

Jay's negotiating position was weak because there was little he could do to force the British to make concessions. The only threat that Jay could make was that the United States might join Sweden and Denmark in an armed neutrality pact to guarantee freedom of the seas to neutral nations—a development that would have hurt Great Britain in its war with France. But what Jay did not know was that Alexander Hamilton, who was strongly pro-British, had secretly assured British Ambassador George Hammond that the United States would never take part in any armed neutrality arrangement, an action that had the effect of greatly weakening Jay's position in the negotiations.[3]

After months of discussion, Jay and Britain's Lord Grenville signed a "treaty of amity, commerce, and navigation" on November 19, 1794. Because of the length of time it then took to deliver news overseas, Washington did not receive a copy of the treaty until the following March. He then waited three months before calling the Senate into a special session to act on Jay's treaty. As might be expected, the treaty was not completely favorable to the United States. The British agreed to give up their forts and trading posts in the Old Northwest—but not until June 1, 1796. The West Indies, which Britain previously had tried to close to all American commerce, were opened to American ships, provided they were small vessels of less than seventy tons. On the other hand, the United States agreed to open the Mississippi River to British trade and promised to pay debts owed to the British before the Revolutionary War. Jay's treaty said nothing at all about Britain's much hated practices on the high seas, such as the seizure of American ships and the impressment of American sailors.

The treaty was so disappointing that the Senate, fearful of a public outcry, took steps to keep its provisions secret. For sixteen grueling days in June 1795 the senators debated Jay's handiwork behind closed doors. Washington was keenly aware that the treaty had defects, but he threw his powerful support behind the pact nevertheless in the belief that the only alternative was war. On June 24, the Senate ratified (approved) Jay's treaty, but only after the objectionable provision limiting the size of American ships trading with the West Indies was eliminated.

While the treaty was being debated in secret in the Senate, the newspapers were filled with speculation about its contents, and rumors spread that some of its provisions were less than favorable to the United States. After the Senate approved the treaty by a 20 to 10 vote (a two-thirds vote is necessary for ratification), Washington reluctantly agreed to have it published, without waiting for the British government to ratify it. But even before the president could act, a Republican senator leaked the Jay Treaty to the press.

The public response was overwhelming displeasure with both the treaty and the American who helped conceive it. Copies of the treaty were spat upon and ripped apart, and when Alexander Hamilton spoke in its defense in New York, he was pelted with rocks and left bleeding at the mouth. Jay was accused of being a traitor who had sold out to the British. At mass meetings in Boston, New York, Philadelphia, Richmond, Savannah, and other cities, huge crowds denounced the agreement. Flags were flown at half-mast, and Jay was burned in effigy. On one citizen's fence these words were chalked: "Damn John Jay! Damn everyone that won't damn John Jay!! Damn everyone that won't put lights in his windows and sit up all night damning John Jay!!!"[4]

Public indignation was so intense that Washington waited seven weeks before signing the treaty. Once he did, outraged Americans reacted angrily. The hitherto popular president was called the "stepfather of his country," and the most rabid opponents of the treaty demanded that he be impeached.[5] Thomas Jefferson, Washington's secretary of state until the end of 1793, was incensed. "Curse on his virtues; they have undone the country," he said of the president, and he accused Washington of being in the company of those "who have had their heads shorn by the harlot England."[6]

A congressional appropriation of about ninety thousand dollars was required to put the Jay Treaty into effect. According to the Constitution, all money bills must originate in the House of Representatives, and Republican leaders in the House attempted to use this provision in a last-ditch effort to nullify the Jay Treaty, arguing that the House had the right to accept or reject treaties if appropriations were needed to carry out their purposes.

Since the Republicans held a majority in the House of Representatives, the treaty's opponents saw the opportunity to undo Jay's work simply by refusing to vote the money that the treaty required.

Before the House voted on this important matter, Republication Congressman Edward Livingston of New York asked the president to turn over a copy of all the instructions he had given Jay and all other correspondence relevant to the treaty. The House approved Livingston's motion and officially requested the president's papers.

In less than a week Washington replied. The papers concerning the Jay Treaty were none of the House's business, he declared, and the House was overstepping its Constitutional bounds in trying to undo the treaty. "It is perfectly clear to my understanding," he said angrily, "that the assent of the House of Representatives is not necessary to the validity of a treaty." The president asserted that handing over to the House "all the papers respecting a negotiation with a foreign power, would be to establish a dangerous precedent that would be detrimental to the president's constitutional authority to conduct foreign policy."[7] By refusing to submit any of the requested papers, Washington established a precedent of his own known as "executive privilege." Often claimed as an inherent Constitutional power, this is the privilege that presidents have attempted to exercise when they have refused to appear before or withheld information from Congress or the courts. (Executive privilege was strongly challenged during the administration of President Richard M. Nixon. See Chapter XI.)

Jay's treaty provoked a long, heated debate in the House of Representatives. Federalist congressmen brought enormous pressure on their Republican colleagues to support the treaty for patriotic reasons, stressing that even a flawed pact was better than a hopeless war against Britain. The climax of the debate occurred on April 28, when Fisher Ames, who was mortally ill, delivered an impassioned speech in the House.

Ames pointed out that the British promise to evacuate their outposts in the Old Northwest was a significant concession that should not be regarded lightly. If these outposts were not transferred to the United States, he said, frontier families would continue to be at the mercy of Indian warriors fighting with weapons supplied to them by the British. If the Congress did not approve the treaty, he warned, "We light the savage fires, we bind the victims." Ames dramatically portrayed the possible plight of American pioneers in the Old Northwest: "You are a father—the blood of your sons shall fatten your cornfield; you are a mother—the war whoop shall wake the sleep of your cradle."[8] Ames's speech was so emotionally charged that Vice President John Adams, one of the listeners in the gallery, said there was barely a dry eye in the House.

The day after Ames's address, the vote on the treaty's appropriations came before the Committee of the Whole in the House. (The Committee of the Whole consists of all the members of the House meeting in an informal session.) The vote was a tie, which chairman Frederick Muhlenberg of Pennsylvania, a Republican, broke by casting his ballot in favor of supporting the treaty. This brave action caused an uproar among his Republican colleagues, who charged that the chairman had deserted their party. (A few days later Muhlenberg was stabbed with a knife by his brother-in-law, a rabid Republican, and in the next election he lost his House seat.)

On April 30, 1796, the House of Representatives finally voted to appropriate the funds needed to implement the treaty. Nearly seventeen months had passed since John Jay had signed the controversial document. During that long span of time, it had been fiercely debated in both the Senate and the House, Jay had been vilified throughout the country, and even the first president had been scorned by many citizens.

It took exceptional courage and insight for Washington to initiate this diplomatic pact, and it required much patience and perseverance to continue supporting the treaty in the face of such widespread and prolonged opposition. For the United States, the treaty's existence was more important than the details of its provisions; only eleven years after granting independence to the Americans, Great Britain had agreed to meet the United States on equal terms and sign a pact with its former colonies. The Jay Treaty postponed war with Britain for eighteen years—until a time when the United States was stronger, wealthier, and in a position to defend its interests much more adequately.

ANDREW JACKSON

BANK OF THE UNITED STATES

In 1791, early in George Washington's administration, Congress established a central bank, the Bank of the United States (BUS). It performed many useful functions. The bank's chief office in the nation's capital and its branch offices provided places where taxes could be paid and where the government could deposit its funds. The BUS aided interstate commerce because it could transfer money for the government, companies, and individuals. If, for example, a company wanted to send money from Pennsylvania to Georgia, it could request that funds deposited in the Philadelphia branch be paid in Atlanta. The new bank also issued bank notes that were backed by specie (gold and silver coin). These notes circulated throughout all the states, constituting the country's first national currency.

The Bank of the United States was given a twenty-year charter. It was privately owned and managed, with 80 percent of its stock held by private individuals and 20 percent by the federal government. The bank began operations with a capital of $10 million.

Jeffersonian Republicans challenged the creation of a national bank, claiming that there was no provision in the Consitution for such an institution and that its establishment represented the unwarranted expansion of federal power over the states. In 1811, Republicans, who then controlled both the executive and legislative branches of the national government, allowed the bank's charter to expire, shortly before the United States went to war against Great Britain. Without the BUS, the country's economy became dependent on notes issued by banks—many without sufficient capital—chartered by the various states. These state bank notes usually were accepted at face value only in the areas where they had been issued. As the lower-valued bank notes flooded the country, interstate commerce suffered enormously. Without a central bank, the federal government found that it had great difficulty financing the War of 1812.

So in 1816, Congress enacted legislation to establish the Second Bank of the United States. Modeled after the first one, the second bank had a total capital of $35 million—three and one-half times the amount of the original bank—and a charter that was to run for twenty years. But the creation of the second national bank did not end the dispute between the supporters and opponents of this financial institution.

During the 1820s, the Jeffersonian Republicans split into two factions. One faction was called the National Republican party, and the other the Democratic party. The National Republicans, led by Henry Clay of Kentucky and Daniel Webster of Massachusetts, generally favored the BUS, while a large number of Democrats, including the exceptionally popular Andrew Jackson, vigorously opposed it.

Jackson was elected president in 1828. The following year, in his first annual message to Congress, he spoke out against the bank and urged a congressional investigation of its operations. Jackson portrayed the BUS as a "national monster" and claimed it was managed by its wealthy president, Nicholas Biddle of Philadelphia, for the sole benefit of the manufacturing and commercial

interests of the Northeast, to the detriment of the government and the farmers of the South and West. The president accused the BUS of monopolizing the banking
industry and of selling much of its stock to foreign invest-
ors. He charged that the national bank extended loans
too freely to its rich patrons while readily foreclosing on
the mortgages of common working people, thus stripping
them of their homes, farms, and stores. He repeated the
argument that the BUS was unconstitutional, even
though the Supreme Court had upheld its constitutionality in the 1819 *McCulloch* v. *Maryland* case.

Congress was in no hurry to heed the president's
request for an investigation of the national bank. Most
legislators felt they could postpone any action on the
bank's future until its charter was due to expire in 1836.

In 1832, however, the bank controversy once again
came to the forefront of national politics. With Jackson
running for a second term, his opponent, Clay, decided
to make the Bank of the United States the chief campaign
issue. Confident of a majority of bank supporters in the
current Congress, Clay asked the legislators to pass a bill
that would recharter the bank immediately—four years
before the existing charter ended. The wily senator believed that this strategy would severely weaken Jackson's
reelection campaign. If the bill was passed and the president signed it, Jackson would alienate his agrarian followers in the South and West. On the other hand, if he
vetoed it, as seemed certain, the president would alienate
many voters in the manufacturing and business sectors
in the East. In either case, Clay figured that Jackson would
lose so much support that he would be denied reelection.

Clay's rechartering measure passed in the Senate
by a vote of 28 to 20 and in the House by a vote of 107
to 86. As expected, Jackson vetoed the bill, but neither
house of Congress was able to override the president's
veto by the necessary two-thirds majority. "The veto
works well," the president told a friend. "Instead of

crushing me as expected and intended, it will crush the Bank."[1] (During his tenure in the White House, Jackson vetoed twelve bills, more than all the previous presidents combined.)

Clay's strategy backfired at the polls, too. In the 1832 presidential election, Jackson defeated the Kentucky senator in the electoral vote by a margin of 219 to 49. Moreover, the president's veto of the bank bill did not cause him to suffer the heavy losses in the industrial East that Clay had predicted. Among the sixteen states that Jackson captured (Clay won only six states) were New York, Pennsylvania, and New Jersey.

The president interpreted his stunning victory at the polls as a public mandate to destroy the Bank of the United States. Some members of his cabinet, including Secretary of the Treasury Louis McLane, advised him that he had already done enough to hurt the bank and should wait patiently for its charter to expire. But Jackson was determined, and he decided to remove all federal funds deposited at the bank. On September 23, 1833, the president announced that the government would begin removing its deposits from the national bank and place them in selected state banks (called "pet banks" by his enemies).

Since McLane opposed this policy, Jackson transferred him to the position of secretary of state and appointed William Duane to take his place. When Duane also refused to carry out the president's order to remove federal deposits from the BUS, Jackson dismissed him, then moved Attorney General Roger B. Taney to the treasury post. Taney complied with the president's directive, but when Congress convened in 1834, the Senate refused to confirm Taney's appointment. So Jackson had to name Levi Woodbury to be the next secretary of the treasury.

Incensed by Jackson's attempt to kill the BUS, Clay and his followers resolved to strike back at the president, whom they derisively referred to as King Andrew I. On December 26, 1833, Clay proposed a Senate resolution to censure President Jackson for assuming "a power not granted to him by the Constitution and dangerous to the liberties of the people." The debate that followed dragged on for weeks. In a three-day speech, the Kentucky senator charged that the nation was "in the midst of a revolution . . . rapidly tending toward a total change of the pure republican character of the Government, and to the concentration of all power in the hands of one man." Then Clay gravely added that if Congress did not act, "we shall die—ignobly die—base, mean, and abject slaves. . . ."[2] The cheers that followed Clay's speech were so loud and lengthy that Vice President Martin Van Buren, presiding over the Senate, had to order the galleries cleared.

Senator Thomas Hart Benton of Missouri, one of the president's strongest supporters, answered Clay's fiery accusations with a highly charged four-day oration of his own. He declared that Jackson's attack on the national bank was in the best interest of the entire country, and he implored his colleagues not to censure the chief executive because taking such drastic action would be, in effect, "a direct impeachment of the President of the United States."[3]

Benton lost his argument. On March 28, 1834, the Senate voted to censure the president, but the Missouri senator would not give up the struggle. He vowed to propose a resolution to expunge (delete) the censure of Jackson from the official record of the Senate at every session of Congress until it was passed.

With federal deposits being removed from the BUS, its president, Nicholas Biddle, fought back ferociously. "All the other Banks and all the merchants may break," he wrote to a friend, "but the Bank of the United States shall not break."[4] Biddle angrily ordered the BUS to call in its loans and stop lending money. This drastic policy caused such a scarcity of credit that many businesses were forced into bankruptcy, factories closed, and workers lost their jobs. When fearful business people petitioned the president to save the country from a massive depression, Jackson blamed Biddle's ruinous credit policy for the economic crisis. He reminded the petitioners that if one man who headed a bank could bring about such unstable financial conditions, then there could be no doubt that the BUS had amassed entirely too much power. The charter of the national bank was allowed to expire; rechartered by Biddle as a state bank in Pennsylvania, it eventually failed.

While the bank controversy was raging, Jackson barely escaped assassination. As the president was leaving the Capitol after the funeral of a congressman, he was approached by Richard Lawrence, a house painter who was carrying a pistol in each hand. From a distance of about thirteen feet, Lawrence fired a shot at Jackson. Although the percussion cap exploded correctly, the gunpowder failed to ignite. Then, as the president lunged forward to try to strike his would-be assassin with his cane, the man fired a shot from his second pistol, this time within a foot or two of his intended victim. Again only the cap exploded, and no bullet left the gun. (A short time later both pistols were examined and found to be in good working order. An expert on guns estimated that the odds of both pistols not firing bullets were 1 in 125,000.)[5]

Jackson angrily charged that his political enemies had plotted this attempt on his life. But after Lawrence's apprehension, it was discovered that he had acted alone and was insane—his motive, he claimed, was that Jackson had prevented him from becoming king of England. Lawrence was committed to a mental institution, where he spent the rest of his life.

True to his word, Missouri Senator Thomas Hart Benton introduced a resolution in each session of Congress after 1834 to remove the censure of Jackson from the Senate *Journal*. By 1837, Jacksonian Democrats were firmly in control of the upper house of Congress, so, on January 16, shortly before Jackson left the White House, the resolution finally passed. At Benton's instructions, the secretary of the Senate took the manuscript copy of the 1834 *Journal* into the Senate chamber and dramatically drew large black lines around the Jackson censure. Then he wrote on the page in large, bold letters, "EXPUNGED BY THE SENATE THIS SIXTEENTH DAY OF JANUARY IN THE YEAR OF OUR LORD 1837."[6]

ABRAHAM LINCOLN

A NATION DIVIDED

When Abraham Lincoln assumed the presidency in 1861, he faced a crisis of staggering proportions. The United States was coming apart at the seams. Between Lincoln's election in November 1860 and his inauguration in March 1861, seven southern states left the Union and others were soon to follow. All efforts to reach a compromise on the issues that separated the South and the North—slavery the most important—had failed, and the nation was moving swiftly along the path to civil war.

Although Lincoln said in his inaugural address that "there need be no bloodshed or violence, and there shall be none unless forced upon the national authority," the new president also asserted that the government he had been elected to head would not permit the dissolution of the Union.[1] He further declared that the southern states' acts of secession (withdrawal from the United States) were null and void, that the nation's laws would be enforced in the South as well as the North, and that the United States would defend and maintain itself as a Union of all the states. He warned secessionists, "You have no oath registered in Heaven to destroy the government, while I shall have the most solemn one 'to preserve, protect, and defend' it. . . . I cannot shirk from the *defense* of it."[2]

Lincoln was personally opposed to slavery, but at the time of his inauguration he was not willing to go to war over it. He felt differently, however, about the issue of secession. He believed that if the southern states were allowed to secede, it would set a fatal precedent whereby any minority of states could desert the Union whenever it disagreed with the majority. If this were to happen, the United States would soon be fragmented into many small, squabbling countries. "This issue embraces more than the fate of the United States," Lincoln said. "It presents to the whole family of man, the question, whether a constitutional republic, or democracy. . . can, or cannot, maintain its territorial integrity."[3]

Shortly before Lincoln moved into the White House, the southern states formed their own government—the Confederate States of America. Though he believed war to be inevitable, the new president at first took no military action against the Confederacy. But when the Confederates bombarded Fort Sumter, a federal fortress on an island in the harbor of Charleston, South Carolina, Lincoln reacted swiftly and firmly. On April 15, 1861—the day after Fort Sumter fell to the Confederates—the president declared that a state of insurrection existed. He then called upon the Union states to provide seventy-five thousand troops to put down this rebellion. The Civil War thus began without a declaration of war by Congress, which was not in session at the time.

To the amazement of many northern politicians, Lincoln did not convene Congress in a special session— as was his constitutional authority to do—until July 4, 1861. With the nation embroiled in the greatest crisis in its history Lincoln deliberately turned his back on the legislative branch of the government and chose to govern for nearly three months without either help or hindrance from Congress.

There were several reasons why Lincoln side-stepped Congress during the first phase of the Civil War. During the winter of 1860, before he became president, Congress had killed militia bills that would have authorized the call-up of troops to deal with the secession and had voted no appropriations for military preparedness.[4] After the fall of Fort Sumter, Lincoln was determined to put war measures into effect immediately, and he feared that precious time would be wasted if these measures were first debated at length in the House and the Senate. There was even the possibility that Congress might reject some of the president's war policies.

In the absence of Congress, Lincoln exercised unprecedented powers, some of them far beyond anything authorized the chief executive by the Constitution. In addition to asking the states for seventy-five thousand militia troops, he requested another forty thousand volunteers for up to three years of service, increased the size of the regular army by about twenty-three thousand, and directed the enlistment in the navy of eighteen thousand more sailors. These steps were taken even though it is Congress's duty, according to the Constitution, "to provide for the common defense . . . raise and support armies . . . (and) provide and maintain a navy." Without congressional appropriation, Lincoln ordered the Treasury to pay two secret agents $2 million to purchase military supplies, and he proclaimed a blockade of southern ports. According to prevailing international law, a blockade could be instituted only as a measure of war, and Congress had not declared such a war.

In an attempt to suppress any actions that might aid the enemy, Lincoln also suspended certain individual civil rights. In Maryland, for example, a border state with many southern sympathizers, some citizens tried to stop Union troops from moving through their state and attempted to disrupt communications between the troops and the Capitol. So Lincoln authorized the commanding general of the armed forces to arrest without warrant any persons suspected of disloyal acts and to deny them the writ of habeas corpus, one of the most precious guarantees of liberty. (Habeas corpus is an order directing an official who has a person in custody to take that person to court and convince a judge that there is sufficient cause for his or her detention.) During the course of the war, President Lincoln trod on other civil rights by shutting down pro-South newspapers, permitting the post office to intercept "treasonable" correspondence, and seizing property belonging to secessionists.

Many Union supporters were appalled by Lincoln's assuming such extensive powers. Supreme Court Justice Benjamin Curtis believed that Lincoln had established a "military despotism," and abolitionist Wendell Phillips described the man in the White House as an "unlimited despot,"[5] or tyrant. Not surprisingly, legislators were among those most outraged by Lincoln's failure to share his authority with Congress. The sentiment of Ohio senator John Sherman was typical. "I never met anyone who claimed that the President could, by a proclamation, increase the regular army,"[6] Sherman declared. In Congress's absence, the Capitol was turned into a hospital and barracks for federal troops.

To charges that he had made himself a dictator, Lincoln replied that since the very survival of the Union was at stake, he, as commander in chief of all the armed forces, had to take drastic action that would not have been appropriate in peacetime. He used a homespun analogy to illustrate this point. Though human beings want to protect both life and limb, the president pointed out, "often a limb must be amputated to save a life; but a life is never wisely given to save a limb."[7] When he finally addressed Congress for the first time on July 4, 1861, Lincoln defended his rule by decree. "These measures," he solemnly told the legislators, "whether strictly legal or not, were ventured upon, under what appeared

to be popular demand and a public necessity, trusting
. . . that Congress would readily ratify them."[8]

Congress justified Lincoln's statement by acting
swiftly to ratify the decrees he had issued in its absence.
It also passed many other measures designed to make it
easier for the president to prosecute the war. In the
course of its special session, which lasted from July 4 to
August 6, Congress enacted sixty-seven laws related to
the war emergency. During this hectic one-month session, Congress authorized an army of 500,000 men,
voted money for a large increase in the navy, and established the necessary machinery for financing the war by
floating bonds, raising the tariff, and imposing higher
taxes, including the first income tax in American history.

Thus, for a short time the lawmakers appeared willing to follow the president's lead in directing the war
effort, but the worsening military situation soon eroded
the cooperative spirit between the legislative and executive branches. Like the citizens of the North, Congress
was stunned when the Union troops were routed by the
soldiers of the Confederacy at the Battle of Bull Run, the
first important military engagement of the Civil War.
Three months later, they were even more incensed when
the Confederates won another victory, at Ball's Bluff,
near Washington. Congress demanded that the North
mount a mightly offensive against the rebels, but General
George B. McClellan, the commanding general of the
Union armies, refused to launch such an attack. A group
of congressional leaders then visited McClellan's camp,
scolded the general for his inactivity, and voiced their
complaints to Lincoln.

The president was not alone in acting beyond the
limits imposed by the Constitution. By the time that Congress opened its regular session on December 2, 1861,
many members of both houses were convinced that the
legislative branch had to take a much more aggressive
role in combating the Confederacy. Consequently, a

seven-member joint Senate-House committee was established to "inquire into the conduct of the present war." This committee was designed, in effect, to oversee and compete with Lincoln's direction of the war. It probed both military and civilian corruption, conspiracy, and incompetence. It investigated the conduct of military officers and civilian leaders in the Lincoln administration. Dominated by abolitionists, it pressured the president to take a stronger stand against slavery. Committee members traveled extensively, summoned numerous witnesses, made detailed inquiries into the causes of Union defeats, and filled large volumes with their proceedings and reports.

The Committee on the Conduct of the War did its most effective work in uncovering cases of corruption and incompetence. For example, its investigations helped reveal widespread graft and inefficiency in the office of Secretary of War Simon Cameron, forcing President Lincoln to remove Cameron from the War Department and appoint in his place Edwin M. Stanton.

The most famous investigation conducted by the congressional committee concerned Brigadier General Charles P. Stone and his part in the Union defeat at Ball's Bluff. Although the primary responsibility for the defeat belonged to Colonel Edward D. Baker, who had failed to follow instructions (his rashness had resulted in his own death, along with that of nearly one thousand Union troops), Congress demanded a living scapegoat. Stone thus became their target. On the strength of unsupported rumors and false testimony, the committee decided that the general was guilty of disloyal conduct. The evidence against him was kept secret, he was not permitted to defend himself in a proper military court, and War Secretary Stanton ordered him imprisoned without trial. A year passed before the congressional committee even sent Stone a copy of its charges. The general then answered each erroneous accusation with such convincing frankness and sincerity that he was released and restored to his army command—a virtual admission by the government that he had been wrongly treated.

Another phase of the committee's work pertained to government security. With many Confederate sympathizers and southern spies active in Washington, the committee took it upon itself to probe the background and activities of anyone it considered a possible traitor. In this role, it even questioned the loyalty of Lincoln's wife, Mary, who had relatives on the Confederate side, including a brother-in-law serving as a rebel brigadier general. The president voluntarily appeared at a closed committee session to assure the legislators that his wife was not a traitor.

As the war progressed, the Republican party split into two factions. Headed by Lincoln and Secretary of State William H. Seward, the moderate wing of the party called upon the public to exercise patience and caution as the government pursued the war effort and decided how best to deal with the problems involved in freeing the slaves. Led by outspoken abolitionists Charles Sumner in the Senate and Thaddeus Stevens in the House of Representatives, the Republican party's radical wing demanded a more vigorous prosecution of the war, the immediate freeing of all slaves, and a much stronger role for Congress in establishing and directing the government's wartime policies.

The staggering defeat suffered by the Union forces at Fredericksburg, Virginia, on December 13, 1862, moved the Radical Republicans to drastic action. On December 16, in a secret meeting, or caucus, on Capitol Hill, the Radicals decided to force Lincoln to dismiss Seward as secretary of state and replace him with Salmon P. Chase, the secretary of the treasury, an abolitionist who was sympathetic to their aims. Their ultimate goal was to replace the president's entire cabinet with Radicals, who then would govern the country as the agents of Congress, with Lincoln serving as a feeble puppet of the legislators.[9]

Seven Radical Republican senators called on the president to tell him what they had decided. Lincoln was shocked by their arrogance and greatly disappointed that they intended to seize executive power from the president. A friend of the president quoted him as saying, "They wish to get rid of me, and I am sometimes half disposed to gratify them. . . . Since I heard . . . of the proceedings of the caucus, I have been more distressed than by any event of my life."[10]

Seward tendered his resignation when he heard of the caucus, but Lincoln wanted to keep him as secretary of state. The president arranged a showdown meeting of his cabinet (except Seward) and the Radical leaders. When Chase failed to provide any proof that Seward's influence was harmful, he felt compelled to submit his resignation. Lincoln, however, refused to accept either Seward's or Chase's resignation. By refusing to punish Chase, the president did much to soften the opposition of the Radicals within his government. By keeping Seward as secretary of state, he demonstrated that the executive branch would not be dictated to by Congress.

The question of freeing the slaves was less easily resolved. Slavery still existed in four border states—Maryland, Missouri, Delaware, and Kentucky—that had remained in the Union. Many of the inhabitants of these states sympathized with the South. Fearful that the border states might switch their loyalty to the South, Lincoln resisted the demands of Radical Republicans in Congress that slavery be abolished in all loyal states. Instead, he proposed that slaveowners in border states and the District of Columbia be paid by the the government for freeing their slaves. Congress passed such a measure for the District of Columbia in April 1862, but the border states opposed the idea of compensated emancipation, and Congress did not force them to accept the president's plan. Finally, on January 1, 1863, President Lincoln issued the famous Emancipation Proclamation, which pronounced all the slaves in the Confederacy to be free. The Emancipation Proclamation was more of a legal formality than anything else, however, since the only way for the federal government actually to free the slaves was to defeat the South militarily.

As it became apparent that a Union victory was just a matter of time, another conflict between the president and the Radical Republicans in Congress arose. Once the war was over, Lincoln intended to act generously toward the former Confederate states. Most of those southerners who would take an oath of loyalty to the Union would not be prosecuted for treason and would have their citizenship restored. The Confederate states would be taken back into the United States as soon as they had met two conditions: all slaves within their borders had to be freed, and 10 percent of their citizens who had voted in the 1860 presidential election had to swear allegiance to the U.S. government.

The Radical Republicans in Congress were opposed to Lincoln's plan for Reconstruction of the South. They felt that it was much too generous to the South, especially since it was the South that was responsible for the war. They also believed that Congress, not the president, should set the terms by which the southern states would be restored to the Union. Consequently, the Radical Republican leaders Benjamin Wade in the Senate and Henry Davis in the House of Representatives drew up a much harsher Reconstruction plan than Lincoln's. Besides demanding that all the slaves be freed, the Wade-Davis Bill required a majority, rather than 10 percent, of the voters in 1860 swear to past and present loyalty to the Union before statehood could be restored. The bill also forbade anyone who voluntarily had been a Confederate soldier or officeholder from taking part in the conventions required to draw up new state constitutions.

The Wade-Davis Bill passed in both houses of Congress and was sent to the president on July 4, 1864, the final day of the congressional session. Lincoln refused to sign it and applied a pocket veto to the bill. (A pocket veto is a power given to the president to kill a bill without vetoing it, if the bill is presented to the president within ten days before Congress adjourns. In such cases, the president does not formally veto the bill and send it back to Congress, but simply refuses to sign it—puts it in his pocket, so to speak.) The Radical Republicans lashed out at Lincoln's failure to sign their Reconstruction bill. In the so-called Wade-Davis Manifesto they denounced the chief executive, angrily declaring that "the authority of Congress is paramount and must be respected," and that if the president "wishes our support he must confine himself to his executive duties—to obey and execute, not to make the laws—to suppress by arms armed rebellion, and leave political reorganization to Congress."[11] Lincoln did not respond to this sharply worded manifesto, and the issue was left unsettled.

Lincoln fully expected that the disagreements between the president and the Congress would grow even more heated once the war was over, and he expressed deep relief that Congress was not in session when the war finally drew to an end with a Union victory in April 1865. At a cabinet meeting on April 14, he observed that it was "providential that the great rebellion was crushed just as Congress had adjourned, and there were none of the disturbing elements of that body to hinder and embarrass us."[12]

Lincoln had fought his last political battle. That night, he was assassinated by a Confederate sympathizer.

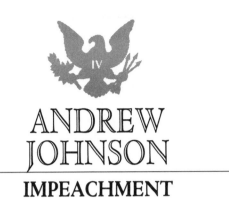

ANDREW
JOHNSON

IMPEACHMENT

Andrew Johnson of Tennessee already had two strikes against him when he assumed the presidency after Lincoln's assassination. Facing a Congress dominated by northern Republicans, Johnson was both a Democrat and a southerner who had owned slaves.

Johnson had become Lincoln's vice president under the most unusual circumstances. In 1864, the leaders of the Republican party had feared that Lincoln would not win a second term unless he attracted a large number of votes from northern Democrats who supported the Union cause. So, for this one presidential election, Republicans and many Democrats loyal to the Union joined forces under the banner of the National Union party, and they sought a prominent Democrat to be the running mate of Republican Lincoln.

One Democrat who had proved his wartime loyalty to the North was Andrew Johnson. A senator from Tennessee at the outbreak of the Civil War, he had valiantly tried to prevent his state's secession, but his determined effort to keep Tennessee out of the Confederacy had not been successful. Johnson was the only southern senator not to desert his seat in the Senate after secession. During the war, Johnson served with distinction as the Union's military governor of the areas of Tennessee that had been liberated from the Confederate forces. Since Johnson had clearly demonstrated his loyalty to the United States, there was no serious objection at the National Union party convention when the Tennesseean was nominated to be Lincoln's running mate. This proved to be a winning ticket at the polls, and Lincoln began his second term with Democrat Johnson as his vice president. Forty-one days later, the untimely death of the president catapulted Johnson into the White House.

Shortly after Johnson became the nation's chief executive, he unveiled his own plan for Reconstruction. For the most part, it was not greatly different from Lincoln's. In order to be readmitted to the Union and elect senators and representatives to Congress, the southern states had to repeal all acts related to secession, cancel debts caused by the war, and ratify the Thirteenth Amendment, which provided freedom for the slaves.

Just as Lincoln in 1861 had served the first several months of his term when Congress was not in session, Johnson dictated his Reconstruction policies from April to December 1865 while Congress was not in session. During this period the new southern state governments were quickly organized, and the president personally granted pardons to many men who had held high positions in the army or government of the Confederacy. By December, when Congress convened again, every southern state except Texas had fulfilled Johnson's Reconstruction qualifications and elected representatives to both houses of Congress.

The Radical Republicans were infuriated when they learned that Johnson had pardoned several high-level Confederate leaders, many of whom had then been elected to Congress. Included in the southern delegations waiting to take their seats in the Senate and House were six members of Confederate President Jefferson Davis's cabinet, fifty-eight members of the Confederate Congress, nine officers from the South's army, and Confederate Vice President Alexander Stephens, who had been indicted for treason. The Republican-controlled Congress maintained that the southern states that had followed Johnson's Reconstruction plan had not qualified for restoration to the Union, and the legislators they had elected were denied seats in the Senate and House.

Another situation in the postwar South also alarmed many northerners, both Republicans and Democrats. The newly formed state governments in the South were enacting laws known as Black Codes, which were intended to give southern whites complete political and economic control over the freed blacks. The former slaves were not permitted to vote or serve on juries, could not attend public schools, and in some states they were not allowed to rent houses or lease farmland. Many blacks were compelled to make long-term contracts as agricultural workers with white landowners, and those without jobs could be arrested as vagrants.

The Radical Republicans were determined that Congress, not the president, would establish the requirements for reconstructing the Union. Representative Thaddeus Stevens of Pennsylvania, who regarded the former Confederate states as "conquered provinces," demanded that "the whole fabric of southern society must be changed" to protect the rights of the emancipated blacks.[1] Congressional leaders formed a Joint Committee on Reconstruction, composed of members of both houses, in order to examine "the condition of the States which formed the so-called Confederate States of America, and report whether they, or any of them, are entitled to be represented in either house of Congress."[2]

Two days after the formation of this committee, Johnson sent a message to Congress, stating bluntly that the Union had been restored and that elected representatives from the southern states were waiting to be seated. In response, Congress declared that no senators or representatives from a southern state would be admitted until both houses had declared that state entitled to representation in Congress.

The first bill that the Radical Republicans pushed through Congress in their effort to dictate Reconstruction policies extended the life of the Freedmen's Bureau, a federal relief agency that provided food, clothing, jobs, medical care, and educational facilities for the former slaves. Johnson vetoed the bill, contending that it was unconstitutional because the southern states that the measure would affect did not have representatives in Congress at the time of its passage.

The House overrode the president's veto, but in the Senate the override fell two votes short of the needed two-thirds margin. Johnson's opposition to the bill cost him the support of many moderates in Congress and caused Senator William Fessenden of Maine to charge that the president had "broken the faith, betrayed his trust, and must sink from detestation to contempt."[3] Later, the Freedmen's Bureau Bill was again passed by Congress, and this time the president's veto was overridden in both houses.

Claiming once again that southerners had been excluded from its consideration, the president vetoed a Civil Rights Bill that promised blacks protection in federal courts. Congress overrode the veto, but there were some doubts about the measure's constitutionality, (the Supreme Court declared it unconstitutional in 1883). So in June 1866 Congress approved the Fourteenth Amendment, which defined American citizenship to include all blacks. It also prohibited states from enacting laws that deprived "any person of life, liberty, or property, without due process of law," or that denied "to any person within its jurisdiction the equal protection of the laws." Two years later the Fourteenth Amendment was ratified by enough states to become part of the Constitution.

The 1866 midterm congressional elections expanded the ranks of the Radical Republicans in both houses, thus putting the president's congressional opponents clearly in the driver's seat. Early in 1867, the first Military Reconstruction Act was passed over Johnson's veto. This harsh measure divided the South into five military districts under the control of army commanders. These military officers were ordered to protect the blacks, enroll them as voters, and begin the process of creating new state governments in the South, which would replace those that Johnson had already recognized.

Congress also took other steps to weaken the president's powers. It greatly reduced his authority as commander in chief of the armed forces by passing legislation directing that all orders he issued to military officers first had to be approved by General Ulysses S. Grant. Distrustful of what the president might do when Congress was not in session, the legislators took the unprecedented step of voting to have the next Congress begin its first session the day after the current session had adjourned. Congress also assumed the authority to call itself into special session at any time—a power previously exercised exclusively by the president.

As the struggle between Johnson and the Congress, which was dominated by the Radical Republicans, grew more intense, the president's popularity in the North declined sharply. But Johnson's cabinet remained loyal to him, except Edwin M. Stanton, the secretary of war and an ally of the Radical Republicans.

Convinced that Johnson would do all that he could to obstruct Congress's Reconstruction policies, the Radical Republicans sought some way to drive him from office. Since Johnson had not committed treason or bribery or broken a law, the Radicals needed to devise a legal basis on which he could be convicted in an impeachment trial. They pushed through Congress the Tenure of Office Act, which made it illegal for the president to remove any federal officer who had been appointed with Senate confirmation unless the Senate agreed to his dismissal. The intent of this new law was to provide grounds for an impeachable offense should Johnson decide to remove the disloyal Stanton from his cabinet without obtaining the Senate's approval.

Johnson and his advisers maintained that the Tenure of Office Act was unconstitutional and therefore not enforceable. Nothing in the Constitution said that the president's right to dismiss cabinet officers required the agreement of the Senate. Since George Washington's administration, the president alone had exercised the power to remove such officers. In the very first Congress, James Madison—the primary author of the Constitution—had declared that this presidential power was "absolutely necessary," and that it was the chief executive's duty to get rid of subordinates whose conduct was objectionable.[4]

On February 21, 1868, Johnson fired Stanton from his cabinet. The Senate then reinstated Stanton, and Johnson, determined to force a showdown on the constitutionality of the Tenure of Office Act, fired him again. The House of Representatives then moved swiftly to impeach the president for "high crimes and misdemeanors." Johnson was indicted on eleven counts, including such vague and flimsy charges as his assertion of authority over the army, his disagreement with Congress regarding the proper course for Reconstruction, and his excessive criticism of the lawmaking branch of the government. But the heart of the case against the president was his willful violation of the Tenure of Office Act.

When Johnson failed to get an early court hearing on the constitutionality of the act he had defied, the stage was set for the most momentous confrontation between the executive and legislative branches in American history. In an impeachment trial, the House of Representatives brings the charges, and its members act as the prosecution; the Senate is the jury, with each senator at the end of the trial voting guilty or not guilty; the chief justice of the Supreme Court presides over the historic proceedings. Conviction is obtained—and the president is removed from office—if at least two-thirds of the senators vote that he is guilty.

After two months of listening to evidence and heated debates, both sides rested their cases and awaited the verdict. The Radical Republicans were certain that many more senators would vote against the president than for him. But seven of their colleagues—all Radical Republicans themselves who disliked Johnson and deplored his policies—refused to commit themselves to voting that he was guilty of the impeachment charges. They questioned whether, in spite of Johnson's errors of judgment, he had intentionally done anything that could be honestly considered a high crime or even a misdemeanor.

The Radical Republicans demanded that the Senate vote first on the charge that the president had violated the Tenure of Office Act, since this was the strongest indictment against him. When the roll was called on May 16, 1868, all seven of the doubtful Radical Republicans cast votes for the president's acquittal. There were 35 votes for conviction to 19 against—one vote short of the two-thirds needed to force Johnson from office. The same results were recorded on the other charges that were voted upon.

The courageous action of the seven Radical Republicans who had supported the president constituted political suicide. Scorned by their Senate colleagues and criticized by many people in their own states, none of them was reelected to the Senate. Yet these men who had placed conscience and duty above personal popularity and political expediency established a very important precedent in the ongoing relationship between the chief executive and Congress: a president cannot be removed from office by impeachment simply because his views and policies are unpopular with Congress and the public.

Radical Republican Lyman Trumbull of Illinois, who had drafted much of the major Reconstruction legislation that Johnson vetoed, explained his vote for the president's acquittal in this way: "The question to be decided is not whether Andrew Johnson is a proper person to fill the Presidential office, nor whether it is fit that he should remain in it. . . . Once set, the example of impeaching a President for what, when the excitement of the House shall have subsided, will be regarded as insufficent cause, no future President will be safe who happens to differ with a majority of the House and two-thirds of the Senate on any measure deemed to be important. . . . What then becomes of the checks and balances of the Constitution so carefully devised and so vital to its perpetuity? They are all gone."[5]

WOODROW WILSON

THE LEAGUE OF NATIONS

Unlike most occupants of the White House, Woodrow Wilson, who had been a professor of political science and president of Princeton University, had written widely about the presidency before he assumed the office in 1913. Believing that the chief problem in American government was the lack of effective cooperation between the president and Congress, Wilson concluded that the president's leadership must be strong enough to provide the unifying force in our political system. Long an admirer of the English parliamentary system, President-elect Wilson wrote to an Ohio congressman that "the President must be Prime Minister, as much concerned with the guidance of legislation as with just and orderly execution of the law."[1]

After his inauguration, President Wilson used various techniques to carry out his role as legislative leader. He began by delivering major messages, such as the annual State of the Union address, to Congress in person, reviving a practice that had not been observed for more than a century. (Following Wilson's lead, all subsequent presidents have appeared in Congress to deliver in person their State of the Union speeches.) The Democrats had a majority of seats in both houses when Wilson, who was himself a Democrat, moved into the White House, and the new president established a close working relationship with the floor leaders in the Senate and House of Representatives. He also met often with congressional committees, sometimes at the Capitol and other times in the White House. Wilson and his staff prepared many of the bills laid before Congress, and the chief executive frequently solicited legislators to support his measures.

Wilson's dynamic leadership and effective collaboration with a cooperative Congress resulted in the enactment of important reform legislation in 1913 and 1914. One act created the Federal Reserve System and reformed banking practices; another act lowered tariffs to make it easier for the United States to trade with foreign nations. Personal income taxes were established to make up for the losses in tariff revenue. Other measures provided a strong antitrust law and created the Federal Trade Commission, which was designed to prevent unfair competition in interstate commerce. In the first two years of his presidency, Wilson skillfully guided more significant legislation through Congress than most of his predecessors had managed to do in complete terms.

When World War I began in August 1914, President Wilson had to turn most of his attention to foreign affairs. For more than two years he walked a diplomatic tightrope, proclaiming American neutrality while supplying England and France with loans and arms and maintaining that Germany—England and France's enemy in the conflict—must respect the neutral rights of the United States to trade with its enemies.

Most Americans did not want the United States to become involved in World War I. In 1916, Wilson was narrowly reelected, largely on the strength of his campaign slogan, which was "he kept us out of war." But when German submarines continued a practice of attacking American shipping, Wilson convinced Congress in April 1917 to declare war on Germany in order to "make the world safe for democracy."

Within months American troops were joining the Allied forces in France and Belgium in the most devastating war that Europe had ever experienced. (The Allies were the United States, Great Britain, France, and Russia; their opponents were Germany, Austria-Hungary, and Turkey.) On January 8, 1918, Wilson appeared before a joint session of Congress to explain his Fourteen Points—the peace program for which the United States and the other allies were fighting. Among the Fourteen Points were open diplomacy to replace secret treaties (secret agreements of alliance had helped draw most of Europe into the war), freedom of the seas, removal of high tariffs that caused artificial trade barriers, and the promise not to saddle the losers with heavy reparations (war debts). Other points included worldwide arms reduction, adherence to the principle of self-determination (permitting people to decide their nationality) in drawing postwar boundaries, and impartial adjustment of colonial claims. The capstone of the president's peace program was "a general association of nations . . . affording mutual guarantees of political independence and territorial integrity to great and small nations alike."[2]

The destructive war continued for ten more months after Wilson announced his peace program. In the end, it resulted in huge losses for both sides, including the deaths of millions of Europeans and about 116,000 Americans. Finally, on November 11, 1918, the defeated Germans agreed to an armistice based on the American president's Fourteen Points. The fighting then stopped; ahead lay the formidable task of drawing up a peace treaty that satisfied the victorious powers.

Wilson was determined that the horror of such a war must never be repeated. The terrible conflict that had just been concluded, he declared, must be the "war to end all wars." The lofty goal of world peace, he reasoned, could be reached if the government leaders who would soon assemble at Paris produced a fair and just peace settlement that included provisions for the foundation of a world organization dedicated to the elimination of future wars.

Unfortunately, the noble mission that Wilson envisioned would never be accomplished. Disagreements with the leaders of France, Great Britain, and Italy regarding important parts of the peace treaty, helped ensure its failure, but another important reason was Wilson's poor relations with the Senate in his own country. These relations were made worse by several errors in judgment by the president.

Wilson's first error of judgment occurred when he urged voters to elect only Democrats in the 1918 congressional elections. The president undoubtedly felt that his position at the upcoming Paris peace conference would be strengthened if the voters returned a Democratic majority to Congress. But his plea tended to make his peace plan a partisan, political issue at a time when strong two-party support was needed. The voters responded to Wilson's call by electing Republican majorities in both houses of Congress. Wilson was thus the only head of state at the Paris peace conference who had to work with a national legislature controlled by members of the opposition party.

The president's second error was the failure to include any prominent Republicans on the peace commission that accompanied him to Paris. Wilson wanted on his commission only individuals who believed in the necessity of establishing a world peace-keeping organization. Though several distinguished Republicans, including former president William Howard Taft and former Supreme Court justice Charles Evans Hughes, shared Wilson's commitment to a league of nations, they were not asked to serve on the peace commission. When the president took with him to Paris only one slightly known Republican, Henry White, he was accused of turning the peace treaty into a partisan issue that pitted Democratic supporters against Republican opponents. Wilson further angered the Senate by not naming any of its members to the peace commission.

Wilson found himself much more highly regarded in Europe than in his homeland. In London, Rome, and Paris, he was greeted by enormous throngs of wildly cheering people; police in all three cities said that no other foreign dignitary had ever drawn such huge, enthusiastic crowds. Because of his promise to put an end to the wars that had ravaged Europe for centuries, the American head of state was hailed by the common people almost as if he were a savior. A deeply religious man, Wilson regarded the outpouring of support from the masses as confirmation that his peace crusade was divinely inspired and destined to succeed.

But the representatives to the peace conference of the other Allied countries were not as idealistic or as optimistic as Wilson. Their nations had suffered staggering losses in the war; besides the huge number of casualties they had sustained, the war had drained their treasuries and ravaged much of the European countryside. The leaders of these nations demanded that Germany and its allies be punished severely for the immense damage they had caused. As a result, many of Wilson's Fourteen Points were either ignored or watered down by the diplomats at the peace table. As a result, much of the Treaty of Versailles (Versailles is a town near Paris) was not to Wilson's liking. Germany was made to pay huge war debts, surrender some of its territory, relinquish its colonies throughout the world, and disband all its armed forces. The treaty said nothing about reducing the armaments of the victorious powers, ending the practice of secret treaties, or removing the high tariff barriers to trade.

But at Wilson's insistence, the final version of the Treaty of Versailles retained the most important of his Fourteen Points: The League of Nations.

Wilson foresaw that the United States would play a leading role in the operation of this new world organization. When he formally presented the Treaty of Versailles to the Senate for ratification on July 10, 1919, he declared, "The League of Nations . . . was the only hope for mankind. . . . It has come about by no plan of our conceiving, but by the hand of God who led us this way. . . . America shall in truth show the way."[3]

Two groups of senators had serious concerns about American participation in the League of Nations. One group of about twelve opponents, called the "irreconcilables," was led by progressive Republicans, including William Borah of Idaho and Hiram Johnson of California. The irreconcilables generally believed in an isolationist foreign policy, meaning that the United States should avoid becoming involved in foreign affairs as much as possible. Fearful that a world organization with the United States as a member could force Americans to defend the interests of such colonial powers as Great Britain and France, they spoke out vigorously against U.S. participation in the league or any similar institution. "I am opposed to American boys policing Europe and quelling riots in every nation's back yard," thundered Johnson.[4]

A larger number of Republican senators, known as "reservationists," indicated that they would support the Treaty of Versailles, including the League of Nations, if certain reservations (limiting conditions) were added that would safeguard American interests. The reservationists' chief objection was Article X of the League Covenant, which guaranteed the territorial integrity and political independence of member nations. (Territorial integrity meant that a nation's territory should remain whole, or undivided.) Article X also authorized the League Council to take action in case of aggression or threatened aggression. These provisions of Article X could, the reservationists claimed, impose unwanted obligations on the United States and make the American government subject to the world organization. Senate opponents of the treaty feared that Article X might override Congress's power to declare war and the Senate's authority to ratify peace treaties.

Henry Cabot Lodge of Massachusetts, the leader of the reservationists, introduced fourteen reservations to modify the League Covenant, aimed primarily at removing any automatic U.S. commitment to league actions. Aside from his legitimate concerns about the part the United States would play in the proposed league, Lodge was motivated by his intense dislike for the president, whom he hoped to humiliate by defeating his peace program.

Wilson felt just as strongly about Lodge. One evening, during the fight over the League, Senator James E. Watson of Indiana asked Lodge what would happen if the president accepted his reservations. Lodge replied, "You do not take into consideration the hatred that Woodrow Wilson has for me personally. Never under any set of circumstances in the world could he be induced to accept a treaty with Lodge reservations appended to it." "But," said Watson, "that seems to me to be rather a slender thread on which to hang so great a cause." "A slender thread!" Lodge exclaimed. "Why, it is as strong as any cable with its strands wired and twisted together." A short time later, Watson met with the president and told him that the only way in which the United States could be brought into the League of Nations was by accepting Lodge's reservations. "Never!" cried Wilson vehemently. "Never! I'll never consent to adopt any policy with which that impossible name is so prominently identified."[5]

Some senators suggested that one way to break this

deadlock was to hold separate votes on ratification of the Versailles Treaty and American membership in the League of Nations. Wilson bluntly ruled out this possibility, asserting that the league represented the heart of the treaty. The president then personally conferred with senators of both parties. He pointed out that if the United States tried to enter the League of Nations under special conditions, every country would have the same right to do so and the result would be chaos. He pleaded with the league supporters to vote against the treaty if it was saddled with the reservations that Lodge had demanded.

Wilson believed that public sentiment strongly favored the treaty and the league. A poll of the nation's press had indicated that an overwhelming majority of newspapers favored American membership in the league, and thirty-three governors and thirty-two state legislatures had endorsed the league. So, though weak and exhausted from months of overwork, and suffering from daily severe headaches, the president decided to take his case directly to the people. Against the advice of his doctor, he embarked, in September 1919, on a lengthy, arduous trip to sell the league to the American public.

For three weeks, Wilson traveled westward, covering more than eight thousand miles and delivering thirty-seven addresses and many more brief statements at railroad stops. His face grew more gaunt and pale, his hands trembled, but in a hoarse voice he repeated to cheering crowds that he had come to fight for a cause, "and that cause is greater than the U.S. Senate!"[6] The farther Wilson moved into the West, the larger and more enthusiastic his audiences became. Alarmed by the size of the crowds he was drawing, the irreconcilables sent two of their best orators, Borah and Johnson, to follow him and speak at the same places he had visited.

At Pueblo, Colorado, on September 25, Wilson delivered one of his longest speeches. With tears streaming down his face, he cried out that the League of Nations was the only real hope for preventing future wars. That night he collapsed from physical and nervous exhaustion; his doctor canceled the remaining speeches and ordered the presidential train to speed back to Washington. A few days later the president suffered a stroke that paralyzed the left side of his body, including his face.

Wilson's condition gradually improved. He grew stronger, his mind was alert, and he recovered sufficiently to walk haltingly with a cane. During his convalescence he did not relinquish, even temporarily, the office and duties of the president to the vice president, and from his sickbed he doggedly persisted in his fight for American entry into the League of Nations.

The first showdown came on November 19, 1919, when the Senate voted on the treaty with the Lodge reservations. The irreconcilables combined with a nearly solid bloc of Democrats—all faithfully following the president's orders—to defeat ratification by a vote of 39 ayes to 55 nays. Immediately afterward, a Democratic resolution to ratify without any reservations failed by a margin of 38 ayes to 53 nays.

Public pressure forced the Senate to reconsider ratification of the Versailles Treaty on March 19, 1920. By this time nearly all the Democratic senators wanted to accept the Lodge reservations in order to ratify the treaty and bring the United States into the league, but many of them still complied with Wilson's plea to oppose the treaty if it was coupled with any reservations. Twenty-three Democrats joined the irreconcilables to defeat ratification by a vote of 49 ayes to 35 nays—7 votes short of the two-thirds majority required for ratification.

Though Wilson was awarded the 1919 Nobel Peace Prize, his dream went unfulfilled. The United States never ratified the Versailles Treaty nor joined the League of Nations. (A separate peace treaty was concluded with Germany in 1921, after Wilson had left the White House.)

World War I was followed a generation later by an even more devastating war. No one will ever know whether World War II could have been prevented if the League of Nations had been made much stronger and more effective by the inclusion of the United States. But the tragic clash in 1919 and 1920 between a stubborn president and an equally stubborn Senate certainly did not advance the cause of world peace.

FRANKLIN D. ROOSEVELT

THE "COURT-PACKING" PLAN

After Woodrow Wilson's presidency ended in 1921, the White House was not occupied by another Democrat until 1933. By that time, the nation was in the midst of the Great Depression, the most severe economic crisis that the American people had ever faced. In light of frightening conditions that included soaring unemployment, numerous bankruptcies, and the failure of many banks, large numbers of anxious voters trooped to the polls in 1932 to register their disapproval of President Herbert Hoover's Republican administration. They elected Democrat Franklin D. Roosevelt, the governor of New York, as their president and sent large Democratic majorities to both houses of Congress.

In his Inaugural Address, the new chief executive discussed the grave problems confronting the nation, and he emphasized the need for prompt, bold, decisive action. Roosevelt warned that if Congress failed to take such action to combat the Depression, he would not hesitate to ask for "broad executive power to wage a war against the emergency, as great as the power that would be given to me if we were in fact invaded by a foreign foe."[1]

Congress willingly joined FDR in his war against the

economic emergency. In the "Hundred Days" between March 9 and June 16, 1933, when Congress adjourned, the president sent the legislators fifteen major bills, and all fifteen were passed. Aimed primarily at relief and recovery, they constituted a comprehensive body of laws affecting unemployment, industry, agriculture, labor, and banking. Never before in history had so many important, far-reaching measures been enacted into law in such a short span of time. Known as the "New Deal," the president's economic program was greeted with enthusiastic approval by most Americans. Though serious economic problems still persisted when Roosevelt ran for reelection in 1936, he won in a landslide, overwhelming his Republican opponent, Kansas Governor Alfred M. Landon, and carrying all but two states.

Despite this popular mandate, the president still faced a huge obstacle to full implementation of the New Deal—the Supreme Court, with its power to declare legislation unconstitutional. Roosevelt wanted the court to recognize the Depression as an unusual emergency that justified exceptional extensions of governmental power, but the justices did not all agree with his reasoning.

Most of the Supreme Court's justices at that time had been appointed to their life terms by Republican presidents. Four of them—Willis Van Devanter, James McReynolds, George Sutherland, and Pierce Butler—were staunch conservatives and foes of the New Deal. Three liberal justices—Louis Brandeis, Benjamin Cardozo, and Harlan Stone—generally supported most New Deal legislation. But if either of the two men in the center—Chief Justice Charles Evans Hughes or Owen Roberts—joined the conservative four, the conservatives would prevail.

In a series of 5 to 4 decisions in 1934 and early 1935, the Supreme Court upheld the constitutionality of several minor New Deal acts. But in a major decision on May 27, 1935, the court declared unconstitutional a cornerstone of FDR's program—the National Industrial Recovery Act (NIRA), which had permitted industry-wide codes that set prices and limited production. Then, early in 1936, the Supreme Court crushed another New Deal cornerstone, striking down the Agricultural Adjustment Act (AAA), which lay at the heart of FDR's plan to help farmers recover from the Depression. A short time later, the court ruled the New York minimum wage law also unconstitutional.

Roosevelt was worried that the Supreme Court would whittle away at the entire structure of the New Deal until it had been destroyed. He feared that next on the court's "hit list" might be the important Social Security Act, which established federal old-age and unemployment insurance, and the National Labor Relations Act, hailed as the Magna Carta of labor because it protected the rights of workers to join unions and bargain collectively.

Angry at the Supreme Court justices, whom he called "the nine old men" (most of them were elderly), FDR sought some means of preventing the judicial branch from destroying his programs, for which he justifiably believed he had popular approval. The president could have waited for one or more justices to retire or die, but there was no way of knowing when this would happen. He could have sponsored a constitutional amendment limiting the court's authority, but such a measure would have required the ratification of three-fourths of the states, which likely would have taken a long time.

Roosevelt had the court problem in mind when he addressed Congress on January 6, 1937. "Means must be found to adapt our legal forms and our judicial interpretation to the actual present national needs of the largest progressive democracy in the modern world," he said. "The judicial branch also is asked by the people to do its part in making democracy successful."[2]

Although he had lost the battle in Congress over his court plan, FDR claimed that he had won the war, since the court had begun to uphold his New Deal programs. Indeed, some historians believe that Roosevelt's court-packing plan was essentially a ploy to nudge the court into a more cooperative position. Yet in another sense the president had lost the war. The court fight had broken the unity of the Democratic party in Congress and led to the formation of a powerful coalition between southern Democrats and Republicans that would plague the Democratic presidents who followed Roosevelt into the White House.

HARRY TRUMAN

THE "DO-NOTHING" 80TH CONGRESS

Franklin D. Roosevelt was the only president to serve more than two terms: he was elected to a third term in 1940 and a fourth term in 1944. Shortly after he began his fourth term, FDR suddenly died of a cerebral hemorrhage; on April 12, 1945, Vice President Harry Truman became the country's new chief executive.

World events moved at a breathtaking pace during Truman's first five months in office. Three days after he became president, representatives of fifty nations met at San Francisco to draft the Charter of the United Nations. The European phase of World War II ended with the defeat of Nazi Germany and Italy in May; in August Truman ordered atomic bombs dropped on the Japanese cities of Hiroshima and Nagasaki, and World War II finally drew to a close when General Douglas MacArthur accepted the formal surrender of Japan aboard the battleship *Missouri* on September 2, 1945.

Aside from the foreign policy concerns that occupied him, the new president faced formidable domestic problems as the nation reverted to a peacetime economy. The same newspapers that carried headlines announcing Japan's surrender predicted that the return to civilian life of 12 million members of the armed forces, coupled with the closing of defense plants, could lead to the unemployment of 10 million Americans. The end of wartime price controls also threatened to cause runaway inflation (an excessive increase in the price of consumer goods). Having served the war effort patriotically, despite their mistreatment at home, America's minorities, especially blacks, demanded better jobs, equal rights, and an end to segregation.

From the beginning of his administration, Truman was determined to follow closely in the footsteps of his popular predecessor. During his first few months as president, he often would point to FDR's portrait and exclaim, "I'm trying to do what he would like."[1] Four days after the conclusion of World War II, Truman presented to Congress a twenty-one-point plan that consisted largely of carrying out Roosevelt's unfinished agenda. It included a series of New Deal–like reforms, such as the extension of the Social Security Act and a plan to help provide full employment for American workers.

Republicans in Congress lashed out at the new president's liberal message. A Republican congressman from Tennessee called it a "fly-specked dish of New Deal hash," and Joseph Martin, the minority leader in the House, declared, "Not even President Roosevelt ever asked so much at one sitting. It is just a case of out–New Dealing the New Deal."[2]

The issue of full employment stimulated the first full-fledged debate on postwar domestic policy. Senator James Murray, Democrat from Montana, proposed a bill requiring the president to prepare an annual report estimating the amount of investment and production needed to guarantee jobs to every American who wanted to work. The Murray Bill then called upon Congress to use the president's report as the basis for voting enough funds to assure that the volume of production would be sufficient to provide full employment.

Conservatives opposed the Murray Bill, arguing that it meant nothing less than committing the federal government to a permanent program of deficit spending (the use of public funds obtained by borrowing rather than by taxation). But a compromise between liberal supporters of the bill and conservative opponents allowed Congress to pass the Employment Act of 1946. The Employment Act created a Council of Economic Advisers to study the economy for signs of weakness and to advise the president and Congress on means of correcting these troublesome signs. The act also created a congressional Joint Committee on the Economic Report to propose measures to stabilize the economy and promote full employment.

Though widespread unemployment did not occur, other aspects of the postwar economy continued to cause serious concern. The legislation that had created the Office of Price Administration (OPA), which had set wartime ceilings on prices and rents, was due for renewal July 1, 1946. That spring, a bitter battle raged in Congress over extension of the OPA. Truman wanted Congress to proceed slowly in lifting price controls, in order to prevent runaway inflation. But a congressional coalition of Republicans and southern Democrats demanded a swift return to prewar conditions, whereby prices of products were determined by the free market rather than government decree. The coalition pushed through Congress a bill that severely weakened the OPA's power, eliminated many controls, and provided for the rapid abolition of others.

Convinced that this bill would stimulate inflation, Truman vetoed it—even though this meant that until Congress could be persuaded to pass a measure that he found satisfactory, there would be no price controls at all. In the first sixteen days of July, the prices of basic commodities—such as meat, corn, and flour—jumped by 25 percent or more, an increase twice as large in only two weeks as had occurred in the previous three years.

On July 25, Truman signed a second Price Control Bill, extending price ceilings on selected items for one year. But the damage had already been done; the new measure was actually weaker than the bill that the president had vetoed. Meat was one of the items placed under the new controls; livestock owners showed their anger by holding cattle back from market. Frustrated consumers, tired of wartime scarcity, waited in line in vain for hamburger at any price. Many blamed Truman for the meat shortage. Finally, in late 1946, the president gave up his fight for price controls, and the OPA was allowed to die.

As prices rose, workers' paychecks shrank. Factories that had paid employees for all the hours they wanted to work during wartime returned to a forty-hour week and stopped paying extra wages for overtime hours. Workers then demanded higher wages to make up for their lost income; when these were not granted, they struck. In 1946 there were about five thousand strikes, an all-time high, and nearly 4.6 million disgruntled workers stayed away from their jobs. Most alarming were strikes involving essential industries—such as steel, automobiles, and coal—that threatened to paralyze the entire economy.

Though Truman was generally sympathetic to labor, he was forced on several occasions to take action against the strikers. A two-month coal strike in the spring of 1946 ended only after the president ordered government seizure of the mines. Truman was then infuriated when, on May 23, 1946, union leaders called a national railroad strike. When the country's trains suddenly stopped, about five thousand freight cars—many carrying perishable goods—were stalled, and more than ninety thousand passengers were stranded. (At the time, railroads were the primary means of transporting goods; a railroad strike therefore affected virtually every facet of the economy.) An irate Truman went before Congress, planning to ask for the authority to draft the striking railway workers into the armed forces. Midway through his speech, Truman was handed a message that the strike had been settled, but the president's dramatic proposal to draft the strikers antagonized many members of Congress and enraged prominent labor leaders.

Truman antagonized another large group of Americans—white southerners who clung to the concept of racial segregation—by staunchly defending equal rights for blacks. When Congress refused to pass a law extending the wartime Fair Employment Practices Commission, the president resorted to executive action that did not need congressional approval. In 1946 he appointed a fact-finding Commission on Civil Rights, which later made recommendations intended to guarantee the same rights to every American, regardless of his or her race or religion.

Southerners in Congress blocked the passage of laws recommended by the Commission on Civil Rights. In one area of equal rights, however, the president again sidestepped congressional opposition, this time employing his power as commander in chief of the military forces. During World War II, the U.S. armed forces had been segregated, but Truman ordered them integrated. He took great pride in the fact that the nation's military forces were almost entirely integrated by the time he left the White House.

The problems that Truman encountered in his first year in office contributed to a sharp decline in his popularity with the American people. His public approval rating in Gallup Polls dropped from a high of 87 percent in May 1945 to only 35 percent by the end of 1946.[3]

Democratic party leaders regarded the president as so unpopular with voters that they advised him to take no part in the 1946 congressional elections.

Soaring prices, shortages of consumer goods, labor resentments and strife, anger of businesspeople and farmers at the effects of price controls, southerners' opposition to civil rights for blacks, and the administration's supposed "softness" on the spread of communism overseas and at home provided Republican congressional candidates with potent campaign issues in 1946. The public responded by electing the first Republican Congress in sixteen years. The Republicans held a margin of twenty-eight seats in the House and two in the Senate. Joined by disgruntled conservative southern Democrats on many issues, the GOP legislators felt confident that they could bury any New Deal–type bills that might be introduced in the upcoming 80th Congress. (GOP, which stands for Grand Old Party, is a widely used nickname for the Republican party.)

The most imposing figure in the new Congress was a Republican senator from Ohio, Robert A. Taft, the son of former president William H. Taft. Senator Taft was the leading champion of business interests and an outspoken foe of many New Deal measures. Praised both by friends and enemies for his unquestioned integrity and zealous hard work, Taft had a distinguished legislative career and earned the nickname "Mr. Republican."

In 1947, Taft and Representative Fred Hartley, Jr., of New Jersey steered through Congress a bill that severely restricted the power of labor unions. The Taft-Hartley Act outlawed the closed shop (which had forced employers to hire only union members), weakened the union shop (under which new employees had to join the union), and encouraged states to pass "right to work" laws which would prohibit the union shop altogether.

Other provisions of the Taft-Hartley Act required union officials to swear that they were not members of the Communist party and forbade unions to use their funds to support political candidates. The act also allowed the president, in the case of strikes that threatened the national economy, as the coal and railroad strikes had done in 1946, to obtain a court order providing for an eighty-day "cooling-off" period during which the workers, under penalty of law, were forbidden to strike.

The Taft-Hartley Act was one of the most controversial measures ever passed by Congress. Union leaders denounced it as a "slave labor law" and regarded the loyalty oath as a degrading attack on their patriotism. By contrast, many businesspeople, claiming that the New Deal had been much too partial to labor, defended the act as a proper attempt to restore a fair balance of power between labor and management. Though Truman vetoed the measure, Congress overrode his rejection, thus providing conservatives with their first important triumph of the postwar era.

Congress then went on to override Truman's veto of a tax reduction bill—the president believed the bill would increase inflation—and four other presidential vetoes. Under such circumstances Truman appeared to have little chance to win the 1948 presidential election. Some Democratic party chieftains even appealed to General Dwight D. Eisenhower, an enormously popular hero of World War II, to be their party's presidential candidate. But Eisenhower refused to run, and the party dutifully but unenthusiastically nominated Truman for another term in the White House. When he arrived at the Philadelphia convention hall to accept the nomination, the president astounded the delegates by announcing that he was going to call the "worst 80th Congress" back into a special summer session to pass legislation that he felt the country needed and wanted. Truman then presented a comprehensive legislative plan that included slum clearance and more low-cost housing, a national health insurance plan, broader Social Security benefits, a higher minimum wage, federal aid to education, strong price supports for farm products, and various civil rights measures.

When Congress, which met in special session from July 26 to August 7, failed to pass any of the president's legislation, Truman took his message—and his campaign for a new term—to the people. In a "whistle-stop" campaign in which he covered more than thirty-one thousand miles and made more than three hundred speeches from the rear platform of his railroad car, Truman repeatedly assailed the "do-nothing" 80th Congress as being interested only in the welfare of the rich and not in that of the common folk. "Give 'em hell, Harry!" shouted a man at a Seattle rally. Truman jauntily replied that he was just telling the truth and the opposition thought it was hell. As the enthusiasm for Truman's message mounted, "Give 'em hell, Harry!" soon became the Democrats' rallying cry.

Still, the odds against Truman's winning four more years in the White House seemed insurmountable. His GOP opponent was New York governor Thomas E. Dewey, a moderate Republican with a proven record as an impressive vote-getter. Moreover, the Democratic party had split into factions. Many southern Democrats deserted the party because of its strong stand on civil rights, supporting instead Governor Strom Thurmond of South Carolina, who ran for president on the ticket of the States' Rights party. Many liberal Democrats broke away as well, choosing to support former vice president Henry Wallace on the Progressive ticket, which advocated a less belligerent foreign policy toward the Soviet Union and other Communist nations.

Though political experts predicted, up until the last moment, that Dewey would win in a landslide, Truman achieved the most stunning upset victory in the history of American presidential elections. He captured 303 electoral votes to 189 for Dewey, 39 for Thurmond, and none for Wallace. To add to the president's pleasure, the Democrats regained control of both houses of Congress.

Early in 1949, Truman asked Congress to adopt his program of domestic legislation, commonly called the "Fair Deal." This was essentially the same group of proposals that he had championed in the 1948 election campaign. The president believed that his triumph at the polls indicated that the public supported such legislation, but once again he was forced to contend with a congressional coalition of southern Democrats and Republicans that could muster enough votes to block some of his programs.

Congress did pass some parts of the Fair Deal program. The Housing Act of 1949 provided large sums of money to cities for slum clearance and the construction of more than 800,000 housing units for low-income families. Amendments to the Social Security Act provided benefits for 10 million additional citizens and increased benefits for retired workers by an average of more than 75 percent. The minimum wage was increased from forty-five to seventy-five cents an hour. The Agricultural Act of 1949 extended the federal government's policy of price supports for certain farm products.

But other important aspects of Fair Deal legislation were turned down by Congress. Truman's request for national medical insurance was rejected. (Medicare for the elderly was not enacted into law until 1965.) Southern legislators engineered the defeat of the president's civil rights proposals. Federal aid to education was rejected when controversy developed over extending such aid to parochial schools maintained by religious groups. And the president's vigorous effort for repeal of the Taft-Hartley Act met with failure.

Truman fared better with Congress on foreign affairs. It approved the president's plea for aid to Greece and Turkey, to be used to fight Communist aggression there. It endorsed the Marshall Plan, which called for huge appropriations to help for those European nations whose economies had been shattered by World War II. At the president's urging, Congress also consented to U.S. participation in the North Atlantic Treaty Organization (NATO), whose member nations pledged mutual military support, thereby reversing a longstanding U.S. policy against joining peacetime alliances. Congress also approved Truman's so-called Point Four plan, which provided millions of dollars in foreign aid to the underdeveloped nations around the world in the hope that such assistance would serve as a bulwark against communism.

Harry Truman has been ranked by many historians as one of the greatest presidents of the twentieth century. Few presidents have dealt with such consistent and unyielding congressional opposition, but Truman's political skills allowed him to turn such opposition to his own advantage with the American people. Several presidents since—most notably George Bush in the 1992 presidential election—have attempted to emulate Truman's tactics when faced with an uncooperative Congress, but for the most part they have lacked Truman's exceptional popular appeal and his farsighted legislative vision.

DWIGHT D. EISENHOWER

THE BRICKER AMENDMENT

After refusing to run for president on the Democratic ticket in 1948, General Dwight D. Eisenhower became the Republican candidate for the nation's highest office in 1952. A tremendously popular war hero who seemed to be above party politics, Eisenhower easily defeated the Democratic nominee, Adlai Stevenson, and helped the GOP regain control of Congress.

Even though they controlled both houses of Congress by only small margins, the GOP legislators believed that with Eisenhower in the White House as the first Republican president in twenty years they were finally in a position to implement a strong conservative agenda. Angered at the way that Roosevelt and Truman had conducted foreign policy without significant congressional input—including Truman's commitment of U.S. troops to fight in Korea without a declaration of war from Congress—Republican legislators now hoped to restore what they regarded as a more equitable balance of powers between the executive and legislative branches of the national government.

Shortly after the 83rd Congress assembled in 1953, Senator John Bricker of Ohio introduced a constitutional amendment that proposed drastic changes in the conduct of foreign affairs. The two most significant changes contained in the Bricker Amendment were (1) to give Congress "power to regulate all Executive and other agreements with any foreign power or international organization" and (2) to require that "a treaty shall become effective as internal law in the United States only through legislation which would be valid in the absence of a treaty." According to the historian Stephen E. Ambrose, the second provision was so vaguely worded that "no one really knew what this meant. Some feared that future treaties would have to be ratified by all forty-eight states."[1] (At that time Hawaii and Alaska had not yet become states.)

The Bricker Amendment had sixty-three cosponsors in the Senate—almost the two-thirds necessary for approval of a constitutional amendment. It also had widespread public support. The amendment was favored by many Republican organizations, the powerful American Medical Association, the Daughters of the American Revolution, the Committee for a Constitutional Government, and the *Chicago Tribune*. Another ardent supporter was the Vigilant Women for the Bricker Amendment—a volunteer organization of housewives and mothers of soldiers overseas—who carried to Capitol Hill petitions signed by over a half-million Americans.

On the other hand, the amendment was opposed by the liberal Americans for Democratic Action, the League of Women Voters, the American Association for the United Nations, the *New York Times* and *Washington Post*, and many prominent Democrats, including Eleanor Roosevelt, FDR's widow. According to one newspaper account, the controversy over the Bricker Amendment had become "our greatest debate about the constitutional ordering of our foreign relations since 1788."[2]

If the popular occupant of the White House had come out in favor of the Bricker Amendment, it very likely would have become a part of the Constitution. But

Eisenhower hesitated to give it his support and asked his cabinet to study the measure before he would make any decision. Secretary of State John Foster Dulles cautioned the president that the amendment would unduly restrict the president's ability to conduct foreign affairs. According to Dulles, the Bricker Amendment would return U.S. foreign policy to the days of the Articles of Confederation, when treaties had to be ratified separately by the individual states. Were Congress to adopt the proposed amendment, he warned, it "would be taken by our friends and by our enemies as foreshadowing a revolutionary change in the position of the United States."[3]

Though candidate Eisenhower had agreed in theory on the need to restore a fairer balance of powers between the executive and legislative departments, President Eisenhower agreed with Dulles and other advisers that the Bricker Amendment would weaken too severely the authority of the chief executive. Eisenhower invited Bricker to the White House in the hope of working out some compromise that would be satisfactory to the senator and him, but the Ohio legislator refused to allow any significant changes in his controversial measure. This left Eisenhower no choice but to oppose the amendment, though, respecting the political sensitivity of the issue, he was reluctant at first to ask other Republicans to join him in opposition. No action was taken in Congress on the Bricker Amendment until 1954, by which time Eisenhower was willing to take the initiative in the fight against the measure.

On January 25, 1954, the president sent a letter to Senate Majority Leader William Knowland, expressing his strong opposition to the amendment. Eisenhower warned Knowland that the amendment "would so restrict the conduct of foreign affairs that our country could not negotiate the agreements necessary for the handling of our business with the rest of the world. Such an amendment would make it impossible for us to deal effectively with friendly nations for our mutual defense and common interests."[4]

But as the debate in the Senate took place, Eisenhower's comments grew less measured. "I'm so sick of this I could scream!" he told his advisers. "The whole damn thing is senseless and plain damaging to the prestige of the United States. We talk about the French not being able to govern themselves—and we are wrestling with a Bricker Amendment."[5]

When the amendment finally came to a Senate vote on February 25, 1954, it failed to receive the necessary two-thirds majority. Even so, the measure refused to die. Senator Walter George of Georgia drafted a substitute amendment, which simply stated, "An international agreement other than a treaty shall become effective as internal law in the United States only by act of Congress."[6] Eisenhower opposed even this version, holding that it still restricted the chief executive's ability to conduct foreign policy, but several Senate opponents of the Bricker Amendment supported the new measure. Even so, the George Amendment fell one vote short of the required two-thirds margin.

Aided by the votes of several key Democratic senators, a Republican president had survived one of the modern era's severest challenges to the chief executive's constitutional authority. Throughout the course of his administration, which lasted until 1961, Eisenhower and Senate Democrats would often cooperate, especially on domestic legislation, demonstrating that many factors other than party allegiances play a role in determining the nature of the relationship between the president and Congress.

JOHN F. KENNEDY

CIVIL RIGHTS

When John F. Kennedy became president in 1961, he soon discovered—as every president after him would do—that the coalition of conservative southern Democrats and Republicans constituted perhaps the most powerful voting bloc in Congress. Though members of the same party as the president, southern Democratic senators and congressmen did not share the same liberal agenda—especially on civil rights. On many domestic issues, southerners had more in common with the Republicans than they did with northern Democrats. Even though Kennedy had served in both the House of Representatives and the Senate, it was not until after he had assumed the presidency that he fully realized how much power Congress wielded. "When I was a congressman," Kennedy complained, "I never realized how important Congress was. But now I do."[1]

Kennedy's first skirmish with Congress was waged against the twelve-member Rules Committee in the House of Representatives, which had long been dominated by southern Democrats and Republicans. Together, these conservatives could prevent the House from considering any bills that they believed were too liberal. (Each bill must first pass through the Rules Committee before it is considered by other committees and the rest of the House.) They had been highly successful in this endeavor, especially after 1955, when Judge Howard W. Smith, a segregationist congressman from Virginia, assumed the chairmanship of the committee. "As long as Judge Smith was tying up the Rules Committee," explained Congressman Thomas (Tip) O'Neill of Massachusetts, "he was a kind of one-man veto, and only legislation that he supported reached the floor of the House."[2]

The president enlisted the help of House Speaker Sam Rayburn in finding some way to prevent the six conservatives on the Rules Committee from scuttling liberal bills. Rayburn suggested that three additional members be added to the committee, two Democrats (presumably liberal) and one Republican. When this proposal was submitted to the entire House, it caused a storm of controversy. Both those who favored it and those who opposed it predicted a close vote. The measure passed, 217 to 212, with 195 Democrats and 22 Republicans voting to enlarge the Rules Committee. (Just as conservative Democrats sometimes sided with the Republicans, liberal northern Republicans sometimes voted with the Democrats.) Kennedy's legislative agenda had cleared its first hurdle, but other obstacles still loomed ahead.

One of Kennedy's main legislative goals was to extend civil rights protections. While campaigning for the presidency, Kennedy had declared, "If the president does not himself wage the struggle for equal rights—if he stands above the battle—then the battle will inevitably be lost."[3] Such declarations had earned Kennedy the support of African-Americans and other minorities.

In the spring of 1961, President Kennedy met with Martin Luther King, Jr., the nation's most prominent black leader. King asked Kennedy to send Congress a strong civil rights bill that would help bring about equal access to all public facilities, from restaurants, lunch counters, and rest rooms to hotels, ballparks, and theaters. The president was sympathetic to King's plea, but he pointed out that the congressional conservatives had strong weapons at their command. They held the chairmanships of key committees that could kill legislative proposals, and they also could sidetrack bills through the use of clever parliamentary maneuvers, including in the Senate the filibuster (a device by which a minority of senators could "talk a bill to death").

Kennedy told King that since the southern legislators were especially opposed to civil rights bills, all of his legislative goals would be in extreme jeopardy if he tried at that time to promote desegregation legislation. King was deeply disappointed that Kennedy wanted to postpone the civil rights battle in Congress. But the president pointed out that other parts of his legislative program—including federal aid to education, a minimum-wage raise, government expenditures for new public housing, and medical insurance for the elderly and disabled people—would greatly help black Americans.

Before King left the White House, the president assured him that he had an alternative strategy to help African-Americans and other minorities. There were steps he could take against racial discrimination by issuing executive orders that did not require congressional approval. With simple strokes of the pen, Kennedy promised, he would strengthen civil rights.

On March 6, 1961, Kennedy created a new committee to fight racial discrimination in the federal government's hiring practices. Called the President's Committee on Equal Opportunity, the new group was given a broad range of powers to enforce policies that promoted equality in government hiring.

Attorney General Robert Kennedy, the president's brother, played a crucial role in advancing the civil rights movement in the 1960s. His first major effort to help African-Americans came shortly after a Supreme Court ruling that outlawed segregation in bus terminals. In May 1961, a group of young Freedom Riders—young blacks and whites determined to make the South comply with the court's ruling—rode buses from Washington, D.C., to three southern cities, where they were subjected to violence and legal harassment. With southern state officials failing to provide protection for the Freedom Riders, the attorney general, after conferring with the president, sent five hundred federal marshals to intervene and prevent further bloodshed. But some of the youthful crusaders were arrested on trumped-up charges and sent to jail for forty to sixty days.

Infuriated, Robert Kennedy then appealed to the Interstate Commerce Commission for an order banning all segregation on buses and trains and the stations and depots where they stopped. This order was issued four months later.

School integration was one of the most controversial racial issues during the Kennedy administration. Many southern school districts had not yet complied with the 1954 Supreme Court ruling to desegregate their schools. So the Justice Department, at Robert Kennedy's direction, filed lawsuits against some of the school districts that were preventing integration. This tactic resulted in an immediate and sharp increase in the number of desegregated school districts.

In September 1962, James Meredith, a black man, attempted to become the first of his race to enroll at the University of Mississippi. Mississippi's governor, Ross Barnett, vowed to prevent Meredith's enrollment, despite the pleas of both Kennedys and a decree from Supreme Court justice Hugo Black. When Meredith arrived at the university, bloody rioting broke out. President Kennedy nationalized the Mississippi National Guard (put it under federal control) and sent federal marshals and troops to the scene of unrest. By the time peace was restored to the embattled campus, two persons had been killed, scores of marshals had been wounded, and hundreds of rioters had been taken into custody—and Meredith was allowed to enroll.

On November 20, 1962, the president issued an important executive order that represented another victory for the supporters of civil rights. It forbade all racial and religious discrimination in housing built or purchased with federal aid. But to the disappointment of black Americans, at the beginning of 1963 Kennedy once again decided not to seek major civil rights legislation. His decision was based on the same reasons he had given two years earlier—a strong civil rights bill would not pass, it would alienate southern Democrats, and it would cripple the rest of his legislative program.

In February 1963, however, the president did submit to Congress a minor bill designed to support minorities' voting rights and provide federal aid to school districts that began desegregation. He told Congress bluntly that racial discrimination separated the American people, was expensive to maintain, and, "above all, it is wrong."[4] Even so, black leaders attacked the president's measure as inadequate, and the bill failed even to reach the floor of the House or the Senate.

In April and May massive civil rights demonstrations in Birmingham, Alabama, resulted in the jailing of Martin Luther King, Jr., and other civil rights activists. When schoolchildren joined the protests, police set attack dogs on them and blasted them with powerful torrents from fire hoses.

Network television news programs showed the savage scenes. With the American public made graphically aware, as never before, of the brutality that underlay the South's system of segregation, Kennedy believed that the time was now right to introduce a major civil rights bill. On the evening of June 11, 1963, the somber president addressed the nation on television and radio:

> *We preach freedom around the world, and mean it, and we cherish our freedom here at home, but are we to say to the world, and much more importantly, to each other that this is a land of the free except for the Negroes; that we have no second-class citizens except Negroes; that we have no class or caste system, no ghettos, no master race except with respect to Negroes? . . . We face, therefore, a moral crisis as a country and as a people. . . . It is a time to act in Congress, in your state and legislative body, and, above all, in all of our daily lives. . . .*[5]

A week later Kennedy asked Congress for legislation that would end segregation in all public facilities, authorize the federal government to play a larger role in ending school segregation, and provide greater protection for minorities seeking to exercise their right to vote.

Not surprisingly, this sweeping civil rights bill was stalled by southern legislators in congressional committees. It still had not been enacted into law when Kennedy was assassinated in Dallas on November 22, 1963. Speaking to a joint session of Congress five days later, the new president, Lyndon B. Johnson of Texas, said: "No memorial oration or eulogy could more eloquently honor President Kennedy's memory than the earliest possible passage of the civil rights bill for which he fought so long."[6] The following year, as a result of intense pressure from Johnson, Congress finally passed Kennedy's landmark civil rights bill. It is ironic that the most far-reaching civil rights law in American history went into effect when a southerner was in the White House.

Congress had passed some parts of Kennedy's legislative program. Some of the major measures included a comprehensive housing act, an increase in the minimum wage, an accelerated public works act, a trade expansion act that empowered the president to reduce tariffs, and approval of the Twenty-fourth Amendment, which abolished the poll tax in federal elections. But besides delaying Kennedy's civil rights bill, Congress rejected his requests for Medicare, federal aid to education, and a bill to lower taxes in order to stimulate the economy.

In most domestic matters Congress claimed dominance during the Kennedy administration. According to Sidney Hyman, an expert on the presidency, Congress maintained this dominance "in defiance of the President, in defiance of the public opinion he mobilizes, and in defiance of the fact that the sum of all local and regional interests do not necessarily add up these days to the national interest."[7]

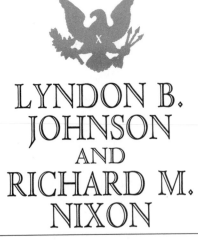

LYNDON B. JOHNSON
AND
RICHARD M. NIXON

WAR IN SOUTHEAST ASIA

As president, Lyndon B. Johnson had remarkable success in getting what he wanted from Congress. Earlier in his career, he had been an effective majority leader in the Senate, and he knew all the various techniques of persuasion necessary to produce the results he sought from the legislative branch of the government.

Besides pushing John F. Kennedy's monumental civil rights bill through Congress, the new president also convinced the legislators to pass other Kennedy measures, such as federal aid to education, Medicare, and a tax reduction. LBJ's own domestic agenda—called the Great Society—constituted the most ambitious program for social reform since Franklin D. Roosevelt's One Hundred Days. Johnson gained congressional approval for measures that ranged from clean water and air laws to the Head Start educational program for preschool children. Another landmark accomplishment was the Voting Rights Act of 1965, which guaranteed that blacks in the South would be allowed to vote, a right that had long been denied them through various racist practices.

In foreign affairs, Johnson at first had the strong support of Congress and the American public. But this support began crumbling in the latter part of the 1960s, and LBJ was virtually driven from the White House in 1969 by a rising tide of protest in Congress and a disillusioned electorate.

The issue that destroyed Johnson's presidency was American involvement in Vietnam, a nation in Southeast Asia. Before World War II, Vietnam had been part of Indochina, a large French colony, but during the war it was seized by the Japanese. When the Japanese were driven out of Indochina in the final stages of the war, the French tried to reoccupy their colony, but nationalist rebels led by Ho Chi Minh, a Communist, fought the French for Vietnam's independence.

As it became clear that the Vietnamese were going to defeat the French, some of President Dwight Eisenhower's advisers urged him to send American military forces to help the French keep Indochina out of the hands of Communists. In April 1954, Eisenhower asked congressional leaders for authority to use U.S. forces to save the French position. Led by Senator Lyndon Johnson of Texas, the congressmen refused to permit American involvement in Vietnam unless Britain also committed troops. The British flatly rejected any plan for intervention, and Eisenhower decided against sending aid to the French.[1]

When the French were finally driven out of Indochina in 1954, their former colony became the new nations of Vietnam, Cambodia, and Laos. An international conference at Geneva, Switzerland, divided Vietnam in two until elections could be held to determine the nation's new government. The United States supported the government of South Vietnam, which after 1955 was controlled by Ngo Dinh Diem. Diem was corrupt and greedy and refused to allow the promised election on the reunification of Vietnam. In a short time, his many opponents in South Vietnam had created the National Liberation Front, or Vietcong, to challenge his regime. Diem received support from the Eisenhower administration, which feared that if Vietnam fell to the Communists, the other nations of Southeast Asia would follow (the domino theory). The Vietcong, meanwhile, received support from the government of North Vietnam, which was headed by Ho Chi Minh.

By the time that John F. Kennedy became president of the United States in 1961, the civil war in Vietnam had intensified, and Vietcong guerrillas were staging successful raids, mainly in rural areas. Kennedy sent approximately sixteen thousand military advisers to help train South Vietnamese soldiers. On November 1, 1963, South Vietnamese generals, angered by the incompetence and corruption of their government, conducted a coup that ended with the murder of Diem. Three weeks later, Kennedy was assassinated.

Historians are still not certain whether Kennedy intended to reduce or escalate American participation in the Vietnam War. In a television interview in September 1963, the president declared, "In the final analysis it is their [the Vietnamese's] war." A short time later, he told another television audience that he believed in the domino theory and felt that the United States should not abandon South Vietnam to its Communist enemies.[2]

When Lyndon Johnson assumed the presidency in November 1963, he faced a difficult dilemma. An expansion of U.S. responsibility for the war against the Vietcong and North Vietnam would divert government funds from his expensive domestic program, the Great Society, and a larger war in Vietnam increased the risk of an armed clash with China. On the other hand, Johnson was a true believer in the domino theory, did not want to be saddled with the charge of having lost South Vietnam, and sincerely believed that if more American military power was employed, the Vietnamese Communists could be defeated.

On August 2, 1964, the media reported that North

Vietnamese torpedo boats had attacked the *Maddox*, a U.S. warship, in the Gulf of Tonkin. Two days later, another attack allegedly occurred. Johnson immediately ordered American planes to bomb North Vietnam's ships and bases and asked Congress for a resolution empowering him to take additional military action to protect American interests in Vietnam. Congress responded with the Gulf of Tonkin Resolution, which stated that the president had the power "to take all necessary measures to repel any armed attack against the forces of the United States and to prevent further aggression."[3]

The Gulf of Tonkin Resolution sailed through the House of Representatives without a single opposing vote. The Senate passed it, 88 to 2, with only Oregon Democrat Wayne Morse and Alaska Democrat Ernest Gruening casting votes against the measure. Morse and Gruening cautioned their colleagues that this resolution gave the president a blank check to use force as he wished in Southeast Asia, but their warning fell on deaf ears.

Johnson used the Gulf of Tonkin Resolution to justify a major buildup of American forces in Southeast Asia, as did his successor in the presidency, Richard M. Nixon. Neither he nor Nixon ever went to Congress to seek additional authority for stepping up military activity in Southeast Asia, nor did either president ever ask Congress for a formal declaration of war against North Vietnam. In 1967, Nicholas Katzenbach, a spokesman for the Johnson administration, told a Senate hearing that the Gulf of Tonkin Resolution was "the functional equivalent of a declaration of war."[4]

Ironically, in 1968, when Chairman J. William Fulbright of the Senate Foreign Relations Committee held hearings to investigate the Gulf of Tonkin incident, it was revealed that the attack on the U.S.S. *Maddox* had been provoked and that the alleged second attack had probably never taken place. The *Maddox* was on a secret intelligence mission when fired upon, and it was sailing within the twelve-mile limit claimed by North Vietnam as its territorial waters. "Lyndon Johnson had participated in a deception," asserted historian Richard M. Pious. "He had suckered the North Vietnamese into the incident, which provided a pretext for the Gulf of Tonkin Resolution, and for the subsequent escalation of the war."[5]

Johnson also deceived both Congress and the public during the presidential election of 1964. Although he was secretly preparing to increase significantly the U.S. role in the Vietnam War, Johnson campaigned for the presidency as the peace candidate. On the campaign trail, he assured the voters that "we are not about to send American boys nine or ten thousand miles away from home to do what Asian boys ought to be doing for themselves."[6] And he depicted his Republican opponent, Senator Barry Goldwater of Arizona, as a dangerous warmonger who would not hesitate to use nuclear weapons in Vietnam. The vast majority of Americans believed their president, and he won in a landslide at the polls.

The huge buildup of American forces in Vietnam started in 1965. By the end of that year, 160,000 U.S. troops had been sent to fight in Southeast Asia. In 1966 this figure rose to almost 400,000. Spokesmen for the Johnson administration kept claiming that victory was within reach, but generals in the field kept clamoring for more soldiers, planes, and weapons. By 1968 American armed forces in Vietnam exceeded 500,000.

As the fighting escalated and the number of casualties mounted sharply, an increasing number of Americans began to protest the war. Antiwar demonstrations, some violent, occurred throughout the country. "Teach-ins" on college campuses lashed out at the concept of risking American lives in a civil war between two groups of Asians. Many young men burned their draft cards or refused to report for military service. Some youths slipped across the border to Canada or journeyed to other neutral countries to avoid service in Vietnam. The longer the conflict continued, the more unpopular it became with Americans.

In January 1968, both the president and General William Westmoreland, the U.S. commander in Vietnam, assured the public that the United States was near victory in Vietnam. Later that same month their optimistic predictions were shattered by a strong Communist offensive during Tet, as the Asian New Year is known. During the Tet offensive, the Vietcong and North Vietnamese troops struck at Saigon, the capital of South Vietnam, and at more than ninety other towns and fifty small villages. Losses were heavy on both sides; after the campaign Westmoreland asked the president for 206,000 more U.S. soldiers. The strength the Communists demonstrated in the Tet offensive made Westmoreland and Johnson's predictions of imminent victory seem absurd. Even some of LBJ's chief advisers, who had vigorously supported the war, now concluded that the cost of continuing the conflict—in both lives and money—was much too high.

Some members of Congress began voicing their concern about America's continuing participation in the war. As the presidential election of 1968 approached, Senator Eugene McCarthy of Wisconsin, an ardent foe of the war, declared that he would oppose Johnson for the Democratic presidential nomination. In the first primary election, held in New Hampshire, McCarthy captured an astonishing 42 percent of the Democratic vote, while a write-in slate of delegates pledged to LBJ was held to under 50 percent. Later that month in a televised broadcast, the president announced that most, but not all, American bombing raids on North Vietnam would be ended. Then the war-weary president stunned his audience by announcing that he would not accept a nomination for another term because of "the divisiveness among us all," and he pledged to spend the rest of his term trying to find a way to conclude the unpopular war.

New York Senator Robert Kennedy, another opponent of the Vietnam War, then entered the race to become the Democratic nominee for president. After winning the California primary election on June 4, 1968, Kennedy addressed his cheering supporters and said he was prepared to debate "whether we're going to continue the policies that have been so unsuccessful in Vietnam—of American troops and American marines carrying the major burden of that conflict. I do not want this," Kennedy asserted, "and I think we can move in a different direction."[7] A few moments later, the youthful New York senator was slain by a Palestinian Arab.

At the 1968 Democratic convention, Vice President Hubert Humphrey, who, out of loyalty to Johnson, had not yet taken a public stance on American involvement in the Vietnam War, became the party's nominee for the presidency. The Republicans chose Richard Nixon, vice president in the Eisenhower administration, as their presidential candidate. In the last few weeks of the campaign, Humphrey began speaking out against the war, but on Election Day Nixon was victorious by a very small margin of votes.

Soon after he took office, Nixon introduced his "Vietnamization" policy, whereby the Vietnamese would be asked to assume a larger part in fighting the war as American forces were gradually withdrawn. Some U.S. soldiers were brought home, but a large number of American troops continued to wage war in Vietnam, and American bombers continued their relentless pounding of enemy targets.

Serious congressional efforts to restrict the president's power to commit U.S. military forces abroad began in 1969 with the Senate's passage of a "national commitment" resolution. It stated that a national commitment "means the use of the armed forces on foreign territory . . . and results only from the affirmative action taken by the legislative and executive branches . . . by means of a treaty, statute, or concurrent [joint] resolution of both Houses of Congress."[8]

But this resolution was never approved by the House of Representatives or the president and did not have the force of law. Nonetheless, it was the opening round in Congress's campaign to reassert its right to participate with the president in any future decision to commit U.S. forces to war on foreign soil.

Shortly after Nixon moved into the White House, he set in motion a plan to destroy the enemy supply lines that the North Vietnamese had established in neighboring Cambodia and to wipe out Communist troops who were moving through Cambodia on their way to South Vietnam. In March 1969, Nixon ordered secret bombing raids on Cambodia. When these bombing raids failed to accomplish the desired results, the president, on April 30, 1970, announced that he was launching a ground invasion of Cambodia to obliterate the camps of about forty thousand North Vietnamese soldiers.

Nixon's move against Cambodia came as an unwelcome surprise in the United States. Just ten days before, he had declared that 150,000 U.S. troops would be withdrawn from South Vietnam within the next year. Now it seemed that the war was about to be greatly expanded. News of the invasion of Cambodia triggered widespread protests; students on about 450 college campuses went on strike. Then, in early May, Ohio National Guardsmen fired on antiwar protesters at Kent State University, killing four students. That same month the extent of antiwar sentiment was demonstrated when 200,000 people converged on Washington, D.C., to voice their disapproval of the government's policy in Southeast Asia.

Despite the unpopularity of the Vietnam War, Congress had, until this point, dutifully passed the appropriations bills necessary to fund military operations. But when Nixon extended the war to Cambodia, the lawmakers struck back at the president. Nixon was made to accept an amendment to an appropriation bill that prohibited the use of funds for U.S. ground troops or advisers in Cambodia. Nevertheless, the bombings of Cambodia continued, while teams that delivered military equipment secretly provided advice to the field commanders on the battlefields.

In 1971, Congress repealed the Gulf of Tonkin Resolution, but Nixon ignored its action. Between 1970 and 1972, each house of Congress passed versions of a measure to restrict the president's authority to send U.S. troops into battle without congressional approval, but they were defeated by the other house. Congress also considered but did not pass various bills to put a deadline on American participation in the Vietnam War.

When Nixon ran for reelection in 1972, his Democratic challenger was Senator George McGovern of South Dakota. McGovern labeled the American entry into the Vietnam War a "dreadful mistake" and asserted: "There is now no way to end it and to free our prisoners except to announce a definite, early date for the withdrawal of every American soldier. I make that pledge without reservation."[9] McGovern won the support of many antiwar protesters, but he lost the election by a huge margin.

Finally, after many months of negotiations, the lengthy Vietnam War drew to an end when a peace pact was signed in Paris on January 27, 1973. The United States agreed to recognize the unity of Vietnam, and the Communists agreed to recognize the right of South Vietnam's government to remain in power pending an election in which all of the people, including the Vietcong Communists, could participate. This election was never held and hostilities between the two Vietnamese armies continued until 1975, when the North Vietnamese finally defeated their opponents. All of Vietnam was united under Communist rule, and Saigon was renamed Ho Chi Minh City.

The United States had paid a heavy price for participation in Vietnam's civil war. About 58,000 Americans had been killed, and 150,000 more had been wounded. Billions of dollars had been spent on the war—the longest and most unsuccessful in American history, and the most divisive such conflict since the Civil War.

After the signing of the Paris Peace Treaty, congressional leaders were determined to limit the president's power to commit U.S. armed forces to combat. In October 1973, Congress passed the War Powers Resolution, which urged the president to consult Congress, when possible, before using U.S. troops in combat, and to report to Congress within forty-eight hours after the beginning of hostilities. Even more important, it required that troops be withdrawn within ninety days unless Congress expressly approved the commitment. And it permitted Congress at any time to direct the president to withdraw troops that had been involved in warfare without either a declaration of war or a specific congressional authorization.

New York Senator Jacob Javits, one of the chief architects of the War Powers Resolution, said that with this legislation "at last something will have been done about codifying the implementation of the most awesome power in the possession of any sovereignty and giving the broad representation of the people in Congress a voice in it. This is critically important," Javits added, "for we have just learned the hard lesson that wars cannot be successfully fought except with the consent of the people and with their support."[10]

As expected, President Nixon vetoed this measure, saying that it was "both unconstitutional and dangerous to the best interests of our nation." Nixon asserted that the War Powers Resolution attempted "to take away, by a mere legislative act, authorities which the president has properly exercised under the Constitution for almost 200 years."[11]

Congress voted to override Nixon's veto. While scholars continue to debate its constitutionality and the presidents who followed Nixon have generally disliked the resolution, it still represents a major step forward by Congress in its effort to reassert its war-making power.

RICHARD M. NIXON

THE WATERGATE SCANDAL

As important as the question of U.S. involvement in Vietnam was, it was only the second most critical crisis of the Nixon administration. The first was the Watergate scandal, which shook the executive branch of the national government to its foundation, resulting in the only resignation of a president from office and the conviction and imprisonment of many of his chief aides and advisers. As this gripping drama unfolded—over a period of more than two years—the other two branches of the federal government also played major roles. In the judicial branch, a grand jury drew up indictments (formal criminal charges); a persevering U.S. District Court judge, John J. Sirica, tried the criminal cases; and the Supreme Court decided whether the president had to surrender key evidence that he wanted to keep secret. In the legislative branch, a special Senate subcommittee was set up to investigate the scandal, and the House Judiciary Committee ultimately had to determine whether the president had committed impeachable offenses.

To direct Nixon's reelection campaign in 1972, the Committee to Reelect the President (CREEP) was established. It included some of Nixon's most capable associates, and it was headed by Nixon's former law partner, John N. Mitchell, who had resigned as attorney general to run the president's campaign.

Before dawn on June 17, 1972, five men broke into the Washington, D.C., offices of the Democratic National Committee, which were located in an apartment-office building complex known as the Watergate. The men were carrying electronic surveillance equipment and wearing surgical gloves. They had been sent to repair previously planted "bugs" in the offices and to photograph any evidence which might prove damaging to the Democratic presidential campaign. Hiding across the street in a motel were two other conspirators, E. Howard Hunt and G. Gordon Liddy.

Because of the alertness of a Watergate security guard and the police, the five burglars were arrested. Initially, the media reported the incident as a routine crime story, and White House spokesmen dismissed it as a "third-rate burglary attempt." But behind the scene, operatives in both the White House and CREEP were scurrying to put into place a massive cover-up intended to mask the most serious scandal in American history. They were successful in concealing its most sordid aspects until after the presidential election in November, and Nixon was reelected to a second term, defeating Democrat George McGovern in a landslide.

But investigative reporters, especially Bob Woodward and Carl Bernstein of the *Washington Post*, would not let the Watergate story die. They discovered that the burglars had ties to the Committee to Reelect the President, and one of them, James W. McCord, was CREEP's security chief. Hunt and Liddy also were identified as working for CREEP. In January 1973, the seven defendants were found guilty of burglary, conspiracy, and wiretapping violations, and later they were sentenced to prison terms.

At first the Watergate conspirators remained silent

when asked whether their crime could be linked to others in CREEP or the White House. (Later, it was learned that they were being bribed and told that presidential pardons would be considered if they kept quiet about the White House's role.) In March, McCord came forth with a damaging statement that pried open the lid of the cover-up. In a letter to Judge Sirica, who had presided over his trial, McCord revealed that he and the other burglars had been under "political pressure" to plead guilty and remain silent, that they had committed perjury (lying) at the trial, and that the Watergate break-in had been approved by high-ranking figures in the Republican party.[1]

The media continued probing for information and discovered that Watergate was part of a large undercover campaign financed by a fund controlled by Mitchell. Stories alleged that Nixon's two top White House aides, H. R. Haldeman and John D. Ehrlichman, had knowledge of the break-in and the cover-up. The president at first denied any White House connection, but he could not long withstand the mounting public pressure to rid the government of officials who might have been tainted by the Watergate affair. So, on April 30, 1973, Nixon announced the resignations of Haldeman, Ehrlichman, and Attorney General Richard Kleindienst. He also dismissed White House counsel John Dean—the man who would later bring the most devastating charges against the president.

Meanwhile, the Senate was setting up a special bipartisan committee, consisting of four Democrats and three Republicans, to investigate the entire Watergate scandal. The chairman was Sam Ervin, Jr., of North Carolina, a Democrat and one of the Senate's leading constitutional scholars. In his nearly nineteen years in the Senate, Ervin had sometimes sided with conservatives and sometimes with liberals and acquired an outstanding reputation for fairness and nonpartisanship.

The vice chairman of the committee was Howard H. Baker, Jr., of Tennessee, a Republican. Like Ervin, Baker was highly respected by his colleagues. While serving on the committee, he did not permit his party affiliation to impede his search for the truth. Before the committee called its first witness, Baker said he favored "a full, thorough, and fair investigation with no holds barred, let the chips fall where they may."[2]

The Senate Watergate Committee began its nationally televised hearings on May 17, 1973. Never before had the hearings of a congressional committee attracted such enormous attention; millions of Americans were glued to their TV sets as the fascinating tale of criminal behavior in high places played across their screens. When Nixon tried to prevent his aides from testifying before the committee, Ervin replied, "I'd recommend to the Senate that they send the sergeant at arms of the Senate to arrest a White House aide or any other witness who refused to appear and . . . let the Senate try him."[3]

To combat charges that secrecy implied guilt, the president changed his mind about permitting his aides to testify. Many officials in his administration were interrogated by the Senate Watergate Committee. The testimony most damaging to Nixon was given by his former counsel, John Dean, who appeared before the committee for four days in June 1973. Dean stated with certainty and in great detail that the president had participated in the Watergate cover-up. This shocking disclosure prompted one of the committee members, Herman Talmadge of Georgia, to ask, "Mr. Dean, you realize, of course, that you have made very strong charges against the President of the United States that involves him in criminal offenses, do you not?" Dean replied, "Yes, sir, I do."[4]

Dean had in effect accused Nixon of the crime of obstructing justice, but the committee had only his unsupported testimony against the president's claim of complete innocence. Which man was lying? About two weeks after Dean completed his testimony, Alexander Butterfield, a former White House aide, told Ervin's committee about the existence of a White House taping system, installed at the president's direction. Virtually all of Nixon's conversations in the Oval Office, in person, and on the telephone had been secretly recorded. By listening to the relevant tapes, the Senate committee could learn whether the president had been telling the truth when he insisted he had played no part in the Watergate cover-up.

Public attention soon focused on the White House tapes. Besides the Ervin committee, a Washington, D.C., grand jury wanted to hear the tapes because it had the responsibility of drawing up formal criminal charges against those persons who might have broken laws. A third—and very important—source also requested the tapes. A separate investigation of the entire Watergate affair was being conducted by the Justice Department. The new attorney general, Elliot Richardson (who had replaced Kleindienst), had appointed Archibald Cox, a Harvard law professor, as a special prosecutor for its investigation. Cox was told to collect whatever information he needed for his investigation, and he was promised the full cooperation of the president and the entire executive department.

Nixon turned down all requests for the White House tapes, citing the principle of executive privilege— the precedent set by President George Washington when he refused to hand over to the House of Representatives papers related to the Jay Treaty (see chapter I). Nixon asserted that the right of executive officers to withhold information from a legislative committee or court is an inherent power of the chief executive under the constitutional separation of powers. The president, he argued, must be permitted to maintain confidentiality in his dealings with assistants and cannot be ordered to "open to public scrutiny" private papers and tapes originating in his office. Furthermore, Nixon declared that information regarding the national defense and foreign policy was recorded on some of the tapes and that the nation's security would be endangered if such sensitive information became public knowledge.

Those who were seeking the tapes promised that no national security matters would be released to the public, but the president refused to release the tapes. When Judge Sirica asked Nixon's attorney how the public interest was served by withholding these tapes, the attorney responded, "The public interest is having the President able to talk in confidence with his closest advisors."[5]

Judge Sirica ordered that Nixon must turn over to Cox nine tapes that the special prosecutor had subpoenaed (demanded by a formal court order). The U.S. Court of Appeals upheld Sirica's ruling that the tapes must be surrendered. Then Nixon offered Cox a synopsis of the tapes rather than the tapes themselves. When Cox refused this offer, an infuriated president ordered Attorney General Richardson to fire the special prosecutor. Instead of complying with the president's demand, Richardson and Deputy Attorney General William Ruckelshaus both resigned. The firing of Cox was then done by Solicitor General Robert Bork, the last link in the chain of command in the Justice Department. This tumultuous series of events, which reached its climax on October 23, 1973, became known as the Saturday Night Massacre, and it unleashed a nationwide torrent of demands that the president be impeached or resign.

The next Monday, several members of the House of Representatives introduced measures to impeach the president, and they were referred to the Judiciary Committee for action. In November the House appropriated funds for the investigation of the president and his aides, and the chairman of the Judiciary Committee, Peter W.

Rodino, Jr., a New Jersey Democrat, began putting together the staff required for the task.

As Nixon pondered his next move, it became apparent that the scandal involved much more than just the
break-in. It was further charged that early in the cover-
up the president had pressured the Central Intelligence
Agency to impede and obstruct the Federal Bureau of
Investigation's probe of the Watergate burglary. It was
also revealed that the White House's "plumbers" unit—
so called because its initial purpose was to plug leaks of
information to the press—had burglarized the office of
the psychiatrist of Daniel Ellsberg, a former government
official who had given the press the Pentagon Papers, a
top-secret study of the origins of the Vietnam War. (The
burglars tried in vain to find information in the psychiatrist's files that might incriminate Ellsberg.) Also, the
Nixon administration had drawn up an "enemies list"
for the purpose of using the available federal machinery
to harass and humiliate political opponents. In this regard, the Ervin committee laid bare "an assortment of
executive-branch 'horrors,' centered on President Nixon
and his closest aides and encompassing the illegal use
and corruption of such agencies as the CIA, the FBI, and
the Internal Revenue Service."[6] By early 1974, twenty-
nine people had been indicted, had pleaded guilty, or
had been convicted of Watergate-related crimes. In the
months ahead, even more Watergate defendants would
be found guilty and sentenced to prison terms.

The public outrage resulting from the Saturday
Night Massacre and these other revelations put Nixon
on the defensive. He finally surrendered a few of the
White House tapes, but one of the most critical had a
mysterious eighteen-and-a-half-minute gap on it, which
the White House blamed in part on an accident by
Nixon's secretary, Rose Mary Woods. Experts later concluded that the gap was caused by deliberate erasures.

The president then stalled for several months as he

sought some way to conceal the damaging evidence that the other tapes contained. Impatient with Nixon's inaction, in April 1974 the House Judiciary Committee subpoenaed forty-two White House tapes. The following week Leon Jaworski, the new special prosecutor, sub-poenaed sixty-four presidential conversations.

On April 29, Nixon appeared on national television to announce that he was not submitting the actual tapes to the House Judiciary Committee but would instead hand over typewritten transcripts of only those portions he felt were relevant to any impeachment proceedings. When these bulky transcripts—totalling 1,254 pages—were delivered, members of the Judiciary Committee an-grily declared that they were insufficient because large parts of the tapes had obviously been deleted.

Finally, late in May, Jaworski took the issue of the subpoenaed tapes to the Supreme Court. Nixon hoped that the court would decide that the principle of execu-tive privilege protected the confidentiality of the tapes. "Inherent in the executive power vested in the president under Article II of the Constitution is executive privilege, generally recognized as a derivative of the separation of powers doctrine," argued Nixon's lawyer, James D. St. Clair.[7]

On July 24, 1974, the Supreme Court rendered its landmark decision in *United States of America v. Richard Nixon, President of the United States*. Chief Justice War-ren E. Burger, whom Nixon had appointed, announced that the court had reached a unanimous decision. Burger explained that the court had agreed with the president that executive privilege in most instances was necessary to ensure the protection of communications between high government officials and their associates. On the other hand, Burger maintained, the president's claim to executive privilege did not give him the right "to with-hold evidence that is demonstrably relevant in a criminal case."[8] The Supreme Court thus ordered the president to turn over the White House tapes sought by Jaworski.

Three days later, the House Judiciary Committee voted 27 to 11 to recommend impeachment of the president on the ground that he had obstructed justice by taking part in the Watergate cover-up. All of the Democrats and nearly half of the Republicans on the committee voted for impeachment. Two other articles accusing Nixon of abuse of power and failure to comply with congressional subpoenas were later approved by the committee. The House of Representatives was expected to adopt these impeachment articles, thereby setting the stage for a trial by the Senate to determine whether the president would be removed from office.

On August 5, Nixon released three subpoenaed tapes of conversations he had held on June 23, 1972, with his chief aide, H. R. Haldeman. One of these tapes revealed that only six days after the Watergate break-in Nixon had given orders for the CIA to block the investigation of the burglary that the FBI was launching. This recorded conversation provided the "smoking gun" that the investigators had been searching for—direct evidence that the president had willfully tried to obstruct justice.

Nixon still clung to the slight hope that more than one-third of the senators might vote to acquit him of the impeachment charges, as had happened in the trial of Andrew Johnson (see chapter IV). But when the president conferred with Republican leaders in the Senate, he learned that he could not count on enough senators' votes to keep him in the White House.

Rather than face the stark humiliation of being the only president removed from office, Nixon announced on August 8, 1974, that he would resign. The following day Vice President Gerald Ford was sworn in as president.

The possibility remained that Nixon might be tried and convicted on criminal charges. But one month after he resigned, Ford granted Nixon a full pardon "for all offenses against the United States which he . . . has committed or may have committed or taken part in" during his presidency. Ford said he took this step because Nixon's humiliation of resigning the presidency in disgrace was punishment enough, "the equivalent to serving a jail term."[9] Furthermore, Ford declared, his conscience told him that it was time to end the Watergate saga and restore domestic tranquility to a nation that had suffered the anguish of a long and ugly ordeal.

Ford's pardon of the former president drew a firestorm of criticism. It was charged that a deal might have been made in which Nixon agreed to resign the presidency in return for Ford's promise of a pardon. This possibility caused such a furor that Ford voluntarily appeared before the House Judiciary Committee to deny flatly that there had been any deal connected with the pardon.

Nevertheless, many Americans were angered by Ford's decision to shut off any attempt to bring the former president to the bar of justice. His pardon of Nixon was certainly one factor in causing Ford to lose the close 1976 presidential election to Democrat Jimmy Carter.

For a time, the Watergate scandal appeared to alter the balance of power between the executive and legislative branches. During and shortly after the period when the crimes of the Nixon administration were being revealed, Congress asserted itself more forcefully and applied restraints to what had been called, under Nixon, the "imperial presidency."

The reform-minded Congress passed the War Powers Resolution, intended to prevent future presidents from involving American military forces in undeclared wars, such as that in Vietnam (see chapter X). The Hughes-Ryan Amendment required the president to report all covert (secret) acts to Congress. The Freedom of Information Act provided easier access to documents gathered by executive department agencies, and the Privacy Act permitted citizens to see information about them that was held in federal agency files. The post-Watergate Congress also passed amendments to the federal election laws designed to limit financial contributions of individuals to election campaigns and to provide public financing for a large portion of the money spent on presidential campaigns.

Congressman Thomas (Tip) O'Neill, who was majority leader in the House of Representatives during the Nixon administration, pointed to another positive effect stemming from the Watergate affair. "The whole world was watching," O'Neill said, "and other nations couldn't help but be impressed. After all, when leaders fall, their governments usually collapse as well. But our transition was orderly and by the book, and this [Watergate] period, as much as anything in our history, showed the strength of our great democracy."[10]

JIMMY CARTER

THE PANAMA CANAL
TREATIES

The Republican party paid dearly for its association with the Watergate affair. In November 1974, less than three months after Richard Nixon resigned the presidency, Democrats picked up forty-nine more seats in the House of Representatives and five more in the Senate. The effects of Watergate still lingered in 1976 when the next presidential election was held. Democrat Jimmy Carter, a former governor of Georgia scarcely known outside his state, defeated the incumbent president, Gerald Ford.

Carter had never been a member of Congress or held any office in the federal government. A large part of his appeal as a presidential candidate was that he was an outsider, who had no connection with Watergate or the "wheeling-and-dealing" that occurred often on Capitol Hill. This honest, deeply religious peanut farmer from Plains, Georgia, impressed many voters as the ideal man to clean up the mess in Washington.

While campaigning as an outsider undoubtedly helped Carter win the presidency, his aloof image created problems after he became chief executive. The new president had to operate without any strong political base; he held no longstanding ties with the Congress that had to approve his legislative measures. Unlike Lyndon B. Johnson, his most recent Democratic predecessor in the White House, Carter had no army of loyal supporters in either the Senate or the House. His reserved personality and scolding manner made it difficult for him to make close friends among the legislators. Also, many members of Congress were miffed because Carter appeared to rely heavily on the advice of associates from Georgia whom he appointed to high positions in the executive department even though they had had no previous experience working for the federal government.

Carter's relations with Congress were put to an early test when he decided that his first major foreign-policy initiative would deal with the highly controversial issue of giving the government of Panama an important role in the operation of the Panama Canal and the possession of the Canal Zone. This heated issue dated back to the early years of the twentieth century. After a United States–supported revolution against Colombia in 1903, the new republic of Panama had agreed to a treaty that gave the United States the use and control of a ten-mile section of land across the Isthmus of Panama, on which would be dug a canal linking the Atlantic and Pacific oceans. In return, the United States paid Panama $10 million and an annual fee of $250,000 (raised in 1955 to $1,930,000). The canal, which was completed in 1914, was built, operated, and protected by the United States.

As the years passed, Panamanians grew increasingly resentful of the powerful neighbor to the north that occupied part of their land and pocketed the revenue from canal tolls. One of the issues that angered the people of Panama was that only the U.S. flag was permitted in front of schools in the Canal Zone—on land Panamanians claimed was their own. To ease tensions, it was decided in December 1963 that neither the American nor the Panamanian flag would fly over Zone schools. However, in January 1964 some U.S. students tried to raise their flag next to a school in the Zone, and violence resulted. During the fighting, twenty-one Panamanians and four U.S. soldiers were killed.

In the years afterward, control of the Canal remained an important issue to patriotic Panamanians, and the need to reconsider the arrangements for American control of the Canal Zone became an important consideration. Presidents Johnson, Nixon, and Ford all attempted, without success, to secure new treaties with Panama.

One reason for the lack of success of these negotiations was the high price demanded by many Panamanian leaders. They wanted the United States to withdraw immediately and completely from all Panamanian territory, including the Canal Zone, which Americans continued to regard as being of strategic interest. In addition, such an agreement was unpopular with many members of Congress. Two-thirds of the Senate had to ratify all treaties, and in 1975 a Senate resolution expressing strong opposition to ending U.S. control over the Canal Zone was sponsored by thirty-eight senators—four more than the number needed to reject such treaties.

In 1976 when Ronald Reagan, former governor of California, contested President Ford for the Republican presidential nomination, audiences cheered loudly when he said, regarding the canal, "We bought it, we paid for it, it's ours, and we aren't going to give it away to some tinhorn dictator [Panama President Omar Torrijos]."[1] An overwhelming majority of people in the United States echoed Reagan's sentiment. One 1977 poll showed 78 percent of the people opposed to "giving up" the canal and only 8 percent in favor of such an arrangement. "The canal was a living example of American ability and American strength," observed author Michael Barone. "For many voters, to abandon it was to abandon an important part of America."[2]

Despite the opposition of Congress and a large segment of the American public, President Carter resolved to change the political status of both the canal and the Canal Zone. "I believed that a new treaty was necessary," the president wrote in his memoirs. "I was convinced that we needed to correct an injustice."[3]

Besides the moral obligation to restore land in Panama to its rightful owner, Carter feared that the canal was in serious danger from direct attack and sabotage unless a new agreement could be forged. Military advisers informed the president that if fighting broke out between Panama and the United States, a force of at least 100,000 troops would be needed to defend the canal, and even that number of soldiers could not guarantee its safety in a hostile environment. Furthermore, Carter knew that reaching an accord with Panama could improve U.S. relations with other Latin American countries, who often regarded their northern neighbor as a bully.

Many months of painstaking negotiations and sometimes angry exchanges were required before the United States and Panama could reach agreements satisfactory to both countries. Finally, two new treaties were completed. The first treaty returned most of the Canal Zone territory to the Panamanians immediately and allowed them to assume limited responsibility for the operation and maintenance of the canal. On December 31, 1999, Panama would assume full control of the canal. The second treaty—called the neutrality treaty—retained for the United States the permanent right to send military forces to Panama after the year 2000 to defend the canal from any external threat that might interfere with its continued use. In time of war, U.S. vessels always would be guaranteed the right to move through the canal.

The Panama treaties represented President Carter's first diplomatic victory in the international arena. He had accomplished in less than eight months what had eluded his White House predecessors for thirteen years. The

Panama treaties were signed by Presidents Carter and Torrijos on September 7, 1977, in the presence of representatives of twenty-six nations of the Western Hemisphere.

But the battle for the treaties had just begun. Still to come in Panama was a national referendum in which the citizens voted whether to accept the treaties. In the United States, the Senate would have to ratify the treaties, and then both houses of Congress would have to pass bills designed to implement (carry out) certain provisions of the agreements.

The Panamanians voted by a sweeping majority of 470,000 to 230,000 to approve the treaties. But these agreements faced an uncertain future in the U.S. Congress. Carter's advisers told him that only 37 senators could be counted on to support the treaties, while 25 were opposed. Of the undeciding 38, a minimum of 30 had to vote in favor of ratification for the treaties to go into effect. "I knew that we were sure to face a terrible political fight in Congress," Carter later said, but he felt that achieving this mission was worth all the effort it entailed.[4]

Ratification of the Panama treaties was not a strictly partisan issue. Former President Ford urged his Republican friends in the Senate to vote for the treaties, and some of them did. Another powerful Republican, Senate Minority Leader Howard Baker, spoke out vigorously on behalf of the agreements with Panama. On the other hand, some Senate Democrats broke ranks to oppose the treaties advocated by the Democratic president.

In mustering support, Carter talked personally with nearly every member of the Senate, and he met with some of the undecided legislators several times. He listened attentively to their objections to the treaties and tried to convince them that the United States, as well as Panama, would be well served by the new arrangements pertaining to the canal and the Canal Zone.

Over a period of many months, the president—who had enjoyed little previous success in lobbying members of Congress—won over doubtful senators one by one. But just when it appeared that the treaties were inching their way toward ratification, Senator Dennis DeConcini, an Arizona Democrat, proposed an amendment to the second treaty, which would have given the United States the right to negotiate for military bases in Panama after the year 2000. The chief problem with this amendment was that it would have required another referendum in Panama.

During the lengthy Senate debate over the treaties, some of the opponents had made harsh, offensive remarks about the Panamanians, which angered the citizens of Panama. So there was no assurance that they would again vote to approve the treaties, especially if a new amendment improved the position of the United States at their expense. Senator DeConcini refused to support the treaties without his amendment. Finally, a compromise was hammered out. DeConcini agreed not to change the wording of the second treaty—thereby avoiding the need for another referendum in Panama— in return for having his amendment added instead to the Senate resolution of ratification.

After weeks of intense debate waged before TV cameras, the Senate, in March and April 1978, ratified both treaties by a vote of 68 to 32. This was only one vote more than the two-thirds minimum, but it represented President Carter's first substantial foreign-policy accomplishment.

The struggle now moved to the House of Representatives. Legislation was needed to carry out many provisions of the now-ratified treaties, including the orderly transfer of property to Panamanians, the relocation of military forces, and a plan for the payment of retirement benefits to the canal employees. After lengthy arguments by both sides, the House voted by the razor-thin margins of 200 to 198 and 204 to 202 to pass the bills implementing the treaties, and the Senate then added its approval to the House measures. Sixteen months had passed between the time that the Senate had ratified the first Panama treaty and the date when Congress adopted the implementation legislation. Carter did not sign the legislation until three days before the treaty took effect and U.S. control of the Canal Zone ended (October 1, 1979).

The controversial Panama treaties had widespread political consequences in the United States. Six senators who supported the treaties were defeated for reelection in 1978. Two years later, another eleven protreaty senators lost their reelection bids. Senator Howard Baker's attempt to win the 1980 Republican nomination for the presidency was unsuccessful partly because he had emphatically favored the new agreements with Panama. And his support for the treaties was one of several reasons why Jimmy Carter was denied a second term in the White House.

No one knows what would have happened if the Panama treaties had been rejected by Congress. After ratification, President Torrijos of Panama said that if the United States government had spurned the treaties, he would have considered ordering the Panamanian National Guard to blow up the canal.[5] Any efforts to cripple the canal could readily have led to a bloody conflict between the United States and Panama.

Instead, the two countries became partners in operating the canal for their mutual benefit. Torrijos paid tribute to President Carter's patient, tireless effort to improve relations between their two countries by quoting Abraham Lincoln's remark that the difference between a statesman and politician is that "a statesman thinks of future generations, but a politician only thinks of the next election."[6]

RONALD REAGAN

THE IRAN-CONTRA AFFAIR

During the last fourteen months of his presidency, Jimmy Carter was tormented by a problem he could not solve. On November 4, 1979, Iranian militants stormed the U.S. embassy in Teheran, the capital city of Iran, and seized sixty-six American hostages. Fourteen of these hostages were soon released, but the remaining fifty-two were held in captivity for months.

At that time, Iran was ruled by a stern dictator, the Ayatollah Khomeini, a fundamentalist Muslim who hated the United States. He stubbornly refused to free the hostages, even though the Carter administration froze Iranian assets in the United States, severed diplomatic relations with Iran, imposed an embargo (ban) on arms shipments to Iran, and even attempted an unsuccessful military mission to rescue the beleaguered Americans. Carter also attempted to open negotiations with the Iranians, but all of these efforts failed.

In the 1980 presidential campaign, Republican Ronald Reagan sharply criticized Carter for not being tough enough on the terrorist regime in Iran. Reagan pledged that if he became president, he never would deal with terrorists—a pledge he repeated again and again after he defeated Carter and moved into the White House.

While Reagan was delivering his inaugural address on January 20, 1981, the Iranian government announced that it had freed the American captives. The embargo on shipping arms to Iran was continued, but the grave concern about the fate of the hostages had ended. It appeared that relations with Iran would not play a major part in the Reagan administration, but events in the president's second term in the White House proved otherwise. In violation of the Iranian arms embargo and the president's proclaimed policy of withholding weapons from all nations that sponsored terrorism, the Reagan administration became deeply enmeshed in the secret shipments of arms to Iran.

Shipment of military equipment to Iran was one component, or phase, of the Iran-contra affair. The second component involved U.S. aid to the Nicaraguan guerrillas known as the *contras* (a shortened version of the Spanish word for counterrevolutionaries). When it was learned that some of the profits from the Iranian arms sales were diverted to support the contras in their war against the government of Nicaragua, the two components became linked in what was called the Iran-contra affair. (A separate book would be required to discuss all the people and actions involved in this complex affair; the chief purpose of this chapter is to show how Iran-contra intensified an ongoing conflict between the president and Congress.)

The taking of new hostages in the Middle East was the reason why Iran again took central stage in White House discussions. Shiite Muslim terrorists in Beirut, Lebanon, kidnapped three Americans in 1984 and four in 1985. As Lebanese terrorists were thought to be collaborating closely with revolutionary colleagues in Iran, Reagan felt certain that Iran had the power to order the freeing of the hostages.

Once the Americans had been seized, Reagan focused on their release. Historian Stephen R. Graubard explained that "in his second term, the President saw the hostage crisis as the all-important one." Even though Reagan thundered and raged, he was as helpless "in liberating the few Americans taken in Beirut as his predecessor had been in freeing the many taken in Teheran."[1]

In August 1985, the Reagan administration tried a new approach to winning the release of the hostages: Iran would be offered the sale of arms in return for the hostages' freedom. To make it appear that the United States was not directly involved in the deal, the first shipment of arms would be delivered to Iran by Israel. The president discussed with his chief advisers the proposal to permit the sale of one hundred United States–built TOW missiles by Israel to Iran. (Israel later would be compensated for these missiles by the United States.) Secretary of State George Shultz and Secretary of Defense Caspar Weinberger strongly opposed the plan.

Nevertheless, two weeks later the first missiles were sent to Iran, but no hostages were freed. When this transfer of weapons from Israel to Iran was later revealed, Reagan first said he had approved the arms shipment, then said he had not approved the transfer in advance, and finally said he could not remember whether he had or had not approved this action before it took place.[2]

Events moved rapidly during the rest of 1985. A shipment of 408 more TOW missiles in September resulted in the release of one hostage from Lebanon. Then, in November, the Reagan administration approved a major shipment of HAWK antiaircraft missiles to Iran, and additional weapons were sent to the Khomeini government through the autumn of 1986.

The two departments of the executive branch of the government that played the largest roles in the secret transfer of arms to Iran were the Central Intelligence Agency (CIA) and the National Security Council (NSC), which consisted of the president's national security adviser and the highest officers in the Defense and State departments. The official most responsible for supervising arms shipments to Iran was Marine Lieutenant-Colonel Oliver L. North, who was deputy director of political-military affairs at the NSC.

The attempt to win the hostages' release by sending weapons to Iran had very limited success. Two additional captives were freed in 1986, but three other Americans were taken in 1986 and four more in 1987. (The last hostage was not released until December 1991.)

Reagan apparently approved some, if not all, of the Iranian arms transfers in the latter part of 1985 and 1986. It was later learned that he had signed specific "findings" for some of these transactions. (A "finding" is a technical term for a presidential order authorizing a secret action.)

When the public first learned of these weapon shipments as a result of a story published November 3, 1986, in a Lebanese newspaper, the president tried to deny that the arms sent to Iran had been in exchange for hostages. He maintained that the arms shipments were arranged to win the favor of "moderates" in Iran who might come to power when the aged Khomeini died. Additional evidence, however, indicated that this was not the case. Lou Cannon, a Reagan biographer, wrote, "Reagan's memory of several key events relating to the arms sales is exceptionally faulty."[3] In March 1987, the president finally conceded that he had misinformed the public. Addressing the nation on television, he declared, "A few months ago I told the American people I did not trade arms for hostages. My heart and my best intentions still tell me that is true, but the facts and the evidence tell me it is not."[4]

Congress had not been advised in advance of either the 1985 arms shipments conducted by Israel or the 1986 weapons sales, which were carried out by the United States. "These sales in themselves appeared to violate

U.S. laws," declared two Maine senators, Republican William S. Cohen and Democrat George J. Mitchell, who served on the Senate committee that investigated the Iran-contra affair and later wrote a book on this subject.[5] Under existing law, the president is required to inform the Senate and House Intelligence committees before any covert action begins. If prior notice is not given, the president must notify these congressional committees "in timely fashion." This provision allows the president some flexibility in those situations when it might not be possible or practical to alert Congress before a covert action commences. However, "in timely fashion" implies a short period, a few days at most. In the case of the arms sales to Iran, no notice was given to Congress until after the bizarre operation had been disclosed by the press, many months later.

Why did the Reagan administration evade the law by withholding this information from Congress? One reason was that the arms-for-hostages exchange was a delicate matter that had to be pursued with great care, and there was always the possibility that a member of Congress might leak information that would jeopardize the negotiations and impede the release of hostages. Another reason for the administration's silence was the fear of angry opposition in Congress if it was discovered that the United States—in spite of the arms embargo and the president's stated policy of making no deals with terrorists—was sending weapons to a country that many Americans regarded as a despicable enemy.

Although the Iranian arms shipments did not begin until Reagan's second term in the White House, the president expressed his concern about the situation in Nicaragua shortly after he became chief executive. In 1979 the forty-two-year dictatorship of Anastasio Somoza had come to an end when his regime was overturned by a guerrilla group known as the Sandinista National Liberation Front. The next year President Carter signed into law legislation authorizing $75 million in emergency economic aid for the new, impoverished government of Nicaragua. Carter said the money was needed to strengthen the moderate elements in the country. However, after his inauguration Reagan indicated his negative opinion of the Sandinista government when he suspended the final $15 million payment of the aid package for Nicaragua that Congress had already appropriated.

Reagan charged that Nicaragua was illegally shipping military equipment and supplies to leftist rebels who were trying to topple the United States–supported government of neighboring El Salvador. Furthermore, the president strongly believed that the Sandinistas, who were establishing close ties with the Soviet Union and Fidel Castro, the Communist leader of Cuba, intended to establish a Communist bastion in Central America that would endanger American interests. So, in the early days of his administration, Reagan sought to make Central America a test case of U.S. determination to draw the line against any further Communist penetration in the Western Hemisphere.

The contras, whom Reagan called "freedom fighters," were the one group in Nicaragua capable of overthrowing the Sandinista government, especially if they had sufficient military and economic assistance from the United States. In March 1982, reports surfaced that the Reagan administration had begun efforts to help the contras. There were mixed reactions to this policy in Congress. On the one hand, many lawmakers agreed that the United States should take steps to prevent weapons from being sent from Nicaragua to the left-wing rebels in El Salvador and to ensure that communism would not gain a foothold in Central America. On the other hand, a large number of legislators were concerned that if the United States–supported contras tried to overthrow the Sandinista government, the United States might be drawn into a "second Vietnam"—a long, costly war with many casualties and unsuccessful results.

In December 1982, Congress enacted the first Boland Amendment, named for Representative Edward P. Boland, the chairman of the House Intelligence Committee. It stated that military aid to the contras could be used only for disrupting arms shipments from Nicaragua to guerrillas in El Salvador. The amendment specifically stated that neither the CIA nor the Department of Defense could use U.S. funds to help overthrow the Nicaraguan government or to provoke hostilities between Nicaragua and Honduras, where most of the contras were based. This first Boland Amendment did not prevent the United States from sending the contras $24 million, on the grounds that all of this money was to be spent solely on interfering with the movement of arms from Nicaragua to the Salvadoran rebels.

Reagan felt the United States should be committed to a much more aggressive approach in Nicaragua; he wanted to provide military equipment and supplies that would help the contras drive the Sandinistas from power. In March 1984, he asked Congress to appropriate an additional $21 million for aid to the "freedom fighters." While Congress was considering this request, it learned that the CIA had helped mine several Nicaraguan harbors. When the mines exploded, some ships were damaged.

This incident infuriated many members of the Senate and House of Representatives. They argued that their intelligence committees should have been informed before this covert action occurred, and they deplored the CIA's part in mining Nicaraguan harbors in direct defiance of congressional restrictions on the funds that had been allocated to the contra cause. Congress then passed the Boland Amendment of 1984, which decreed the cutoff of all military aid to the contras from October 1984 through December 1985. But during this period, the Reagan administration was actively soliciting money from other countries and wealthy Americans to keep alive the contras' offensive in Nicaragua's civil war.

Shortly after the story about covert sales of U.S. arms to Iran appeared in a Lebanese newspaper in November 1986, the secrecy surrounding the Iran-contra affair began to lift. On November 25, Attorney General Edwin Meese made the shocking disclosure that some of the profits from the arms sales to Iran had been diverted to help the contras battle the Sandinista government—without the prior knowledge or consent of Congress. Both components of the Iran-contra operation pointed to the possible commission of many illegal acts. The public wondered whether Iran-contra was a "second Watergate," and the media labeled this new scandal "Irangate."

A series of important events followed in rapid order. Reagan vehemently denied the most serious charge: that he had known or approved of the diversion of funds from the Iranian arms sales to the contras. National Security Adviser John M. Poindexter resigned; his aide, Lieutenant-Colonel Oliver North, was fired. The president named a three-man commission, headed by former Senator John Tower, to investigate the affair. *The Tower Report*, released on February 26, 1987, accused members of the Reagan administration of serious misdeeds and criticized the president for not paying close attention to what his aides were doing and for not asking the kinds of questions that would have revealed problems that might have been corrected.

Meanwhile, an independent consul, much like the special prosecutor in the Watergate scandal, was appointed to find out whether any of the persons who took part in the Iran-contra affair had committed crimes for which they should be tried in courts. A former federal judge, Lawrence Walsh, accepted the position of independent consul. Moreover, both houses of Congress established special bipartisan committees (called "select" committees because they are temporary for a limited purpose) to probe deeply into all aspects of the complicated affair that had grabbed the attention of the entire nation.

The Senate and House select committees decided to hold joint hearings, thereby eliminating the need for the same witnesses to give their testimony twice. During the twelve weeks of televised hearings that began on May 5 and ended August 3, 1987, the Senate and House select committees heard testimony that revealed an almost incredible mismanagement of U.S. foreign policy and the commission of many crimes. The committees reviewed thousands of documents and examined more than thirty witnesses before issuing their reports on November 13, 1987.

North and Poindexter were two of the key witnesses. They agreed to testify after being granted limited immunity. This meant that anything they said in the congressional hearings could not be used later as evidence against them in criminal trials, unless the independent consul could obtain the same evidence from other sources that had not been prejudiced by testimony given during the congressional investigation.

North told a bizarre story that included conspiring with a retired Air Force general and arms merchants in the Middle East to help arrange the weapons sales to Iran and deposit the funds in secret bank accounts in Switzerland. He admitted accepting personal gifts from his coconspirators, even though this practice is not allowed for members of the U.S. armed forces. North discussed in great detail the part he had played in securing arms for the contras. And he told the congressional committees that when he learned that the cover-up of the entire affair was coming apart, he and his secretary shredded many government documents, thus destroying information that might have helped put together the Iran-contra puzzle.

Among the most shocking revelations in North's testimony was his open admission that he had lied to Congress. He said he felt compelled to lie because he did this to protect other people's lives. North explained that he was engaged in delicate, secret operations that posed severe risks for some of the participants. When asked why he broke the law that requires notification to congressional intelligence committees before covert actions are begun, he said that not all members of Congress could be trusted to keep the operations secret.

Despite the appalling misdeeds that North described—often approvingly—millions of television viewers sided with the tall, handsome Marine, who said that everything he had done was carried out in the line of duty. His supporters viewed North as a loyal soldier, following orders and implementing policies that had been handed down by higher officials in the Reagan White House. They felt that he was the "fall guy taking the rap" for the president and his chief advisers. Thousands of letters and telegrams praising North flooded the offices of senators and congressmen. Other witnesses acknowledged that they, too, had lied to Congress, but their admissions failed to generate the sympathy and forgiveness that North received from a large number of Americans.

Admiral Poindexter was not the attractive witness that North had been. Cold and aloof, he answered questions bluntly and repeatedly claimed that he could not remember certain events. But his testimony was extremely important. As North's boss, Poindexter had direct knowledge of the policies and plans that were being contemplated, and as national security adviser he had conferred almost daily with Reagan. If anyone could have told whether the president knew about the diversion of funds from the Iran weapons sales to the contras, it should have been this witness.

Poindexter testified that he had approved of the diversion of funds but did not notify the president of this decision. He told the congressional hearing, "Although I was convinced that we could properly do it and that the President would approve if asked, I made a very deliberate decision not to ask the President so that I could insulate him and provide some future deniability for the President if it ever leaked out."[6] (No concrete evidence that Reagan knew about the diversion has ever been revealed.)

Independent counsel Lawrence Walsh launched a criminal probe of Iran-contra participants that lasted more than five years. By the beginning of 1993, ten persons had either pleaded guilty or been convicted on criminal charges. None of them, however, served a prison term, except one defendant who had not reported on his income tax returns gains related to weapons sales.

North was convicted in 1989 on three felony counts of obstructing Congress, destroying government documents, and accepting illegal gifts. But in 1991 his convictions were overturned after an appeals court judge ruled that the testimony of a key witness had been influenced by his exposure to North's testimony given under immunity at the congressional hearing. Poindexter was convicted on five counts, but his conviction also was overturned when a federal appeals court decreed that witnesses at his trial may have been prejudiced by his testimony before the congressional investigating committees.

The effects of the Iran-contra affair were widespread and, in some respects, devastating. A well-liked president lost much of his popularity, and he never regained the strong approval of the American public that he had enjoyed before the scandal was unveiled. The reputations of some of the chief leaders in the Reagan administration were also severely damaged. The power of the legislative branch of the government was sorely tested. Its laws had been intentionally broken or secretly bypassed. Members of Congress had been neglected in the shaping of foreign policy, lied to, and accused of being unable to keep secret sensitive national security matters.

In their book on the Iran-contra affair, Senators Cohen and Mitchell state, "Though Congress and the Executive may debate and disagree, neither can afford to deceive the other. . . . The struggle for power between the Executive and Legislative Branches is destined to continue. But that struggle, inherent in a system of calculated checks and balances, must be waged in a spirit of good faith, one that recognizes that the responsibilities of each require accommodation, and sometimes compromise."[7]

GEORGE BUSH

OPERATION DESERT STORM

For more than 150 years no president of the United States, on completing his term in office, turned the keys to the White House over to his vice president. In 1837, Vice President Martin Van Buren had succeeded Andrew Jackson in the presidency, but this feat was not repeated again until 1989 when George Bush became chief executive after eight years of service as Ronald Reagan's vice president.

Bush's administration, like those of Presidents Carter and Reagan before him, was troubled by a crisis in the Middle East. But instead of being harassed by Iran and Ayatollah Khomeini, Bush was challenged by the belligerence of Iraq and its dictator, Saddam Hussein.

Iraq had a longstanding quarrel with its southern neighbor, the small but oil-rich nation of Kuwait. Saddam accused Kuwait of exceeding the oil production limits agreed upon by the Organization of Petroleum Exporting Countries (OPEC), thereby helping to drive down the price that Iraq received for its oil in the world market. Iraq demanded that Kuwait pay billions of dollars in compensation for the reduced oil prices, renounce its claims to the disputed oil field that lies underneath the Iraqi-Kuwait border in the area called Rumaila, and cede to Iraq the island of Bubiyan, which controls the entrance to Iraq's port at Umm Qasr.

When he felt certain that Kuwait would not grant his demands, Saddam sent thousands of troops and tanks into Kuwait on August 2, 1990. Kuwait was virtually defenseless, and within twelve hours the entire country was occupied by Iraqis. Saddam's troops were poised on Kuwait's border with Saudi Arabia, and an anxious world wondered whether they would next invade that country—the largest oil producer in the Middle East. The industrial economy of many countries was dependent on Saudi Arabia's oil.

Initially, the Bush administration's chief concern was preventing the Iraqis from moving into Saudi Arabia. When the United States offered to send military help to the Saudis, King Fahd of Saudi Arabia at first was hesitant about permitting American or other foreign troops on his soil. He said he preferred to work within the Arab League to find a solution to the problems posed by Iraqi soldiers on his country's border. No one could have predicted Saddam's next move, but King Fahd doubted that he would attack Saudi Arabia. Some officials in the United States government also were not convinced that Saddam planned to carry his war of conquest beyond Kuwait. Both the CIA and the Defense Intelligence Agency believed it unlikely that Iraq would invade Saudi Arabia.[1] Nevertheless, the Bush administration finally convinced King Fahd that his people were in grave danger if he did not accept military aid from the United States and other countries.

When Bush addressed the nation on television on August 8, 1990, he declared that "a line has been drawn in the sand" and that Iraq's aggression would not be tolerated. He told the American public that there must be an unconditional and complete withdrawal of all Iraqi forces from Kuwait, and that he was sending U.S. troops and weapons to Saudi Arabia as part of a multinational force that would protect the Saudis.

The United Nations also was quick to respond to Saddam's belligerent action. On August 6, the UN Security Council voted 13 to 0, with Cuba and Yemen abstaining, to impose stringent economic sanctions on Iraq. Shipments of nearly all products to Iraq would be prohibited, and Iraq would not be permitted to sell its oil on the world market. The purpose of these embargoes was to paralyze Iraq's entire economy. Later in August, the Security Council voted to stop and inspect all Iraqi ships.

As American armed forces and military equipment started moving to Saudi Arabia, Bush worked tirelessly to forge a coalition of nations opposed to Iraq's aggression. The Soviet Union—the United States' chief adversary during more than four decades of the Cold War—condemned Saddam Hussein's actions and tried to pressure him to free Kuwait. Most of the Arab countries joined the anti-Iraq coalition and accepted Israel as an ally, thus bringing together on the same side Muslims and Jews who had long been enemies. Great Britain and France sent large numbers of soldiers, planes, ships, and weapons to Saudi Arabia and the Persian Gulf. Germany and Japan pledged billions of dollars to help pay for the expensive military operations.

In the early days of the crisis, it was widely believed that the economic sanctions would force Saddam to back down when he became fully aware of the damaging effects of an international quarantine that would shut off Iraq's imports and exports. "Economic sanctions, if fully enforced," Bush declared, "can be very, very effective. . . . [They] should begin to bite pretty soon."[2] As late as October 1990, both General Colin L. Powell, the chairman of the joint chiefs of staff, and General H. Norman Schwarzkopf, the American field commander in

Saudi Arabia, still believed that the economic sanctions might force Saddam to withdraw his troops from Kuwait.[3]

The American public, according to polls, overwhelmingly approved of Bush's decision to send troops to Saudi Arabia. In late September, both the Senate and the House passed resolutions supporting the president's actions to that point. Only three senators, Democrats Bob Kerrey and Edward Kennedy and Republican Mark Hatfield, voted against the resolution.

In early November, with more than 200,000 U.S. troops already in the Middle East, Bush ordered an even larger buildup of American forces in the Gulf area. Having decided that economic sanctions were working too slowly in producing the desired results, the Bush administration was preparing to undertake an offensive campaign against Iraq. It appeared that "Desert Shield" soon would be replaced by "Desert Storm."

Many legislators were concerned that the president would initiate hostilities in the Middle East without first securing the approval of Congress. This brought into sharp focus the longstanding legal dilemma arising from two competing clauses in the Constitution. One clause says that Congress alone has the power to declare war; another clause says that the president shall be the commander in chief of the army and navy. James Madison, a key framer of the Constitution who later became president, tried to explain this dilemma. "The Constitution supposes what the history of all governments demonstrates," he wrote in 1798, "that the Executive is the branch of power most interested in war and prone to it. It has accordingly with studied care vested the question of war in the Legislature."[4]

Secretary of Defense Dick Cheney told the Senate Armed Services Committee that he did not believe that the president required any additional authorization from Congress to send Americans into battle. "The President, as Commander in Chief," he said, "has the authority to commit U.S. forces."[5] White House staff members pointed out more than two hundred examples of presidents sending military personnel to foreign battlefields, yet Congress has formally declared war only five times, most recently in 1941 after the Japanese attacked Pearl Harbor. This interpretation of the war-making authority was challenged by many members of Congress, including Senate Majority Leader George J. Mitchell, who steadfastly maintained that while the president "doesn't need the approval of Congress to *threaten* war, he does need the approval of Congress to *make* war."[6]

The Senate Armed Services Committee summoned military and political experts to testify about American policy in the Iraqi dispute. Two former chairmen of the joint chiefs of staff, General David C. Jones and Admiral William J. Crowe, Jr., favored a cautious approach. Referring to the recent massive buildup of U.S. forces in the Persian Gulf area, General Jones said, "My main concern with this latest scheduled reinforcement isn't that we might choose to fight but rather that the deployment might cause us to fight, perhaps prematurely and perhaps unnecessarily."[7] Admiral Crowe told the Senate committee that maintaining the pressure of UN economic sanctions was the best way to deal with the current situation. "The issue is not whether an embargo will work," he asserted, "but whether we have the patience to let it take effect."[8]

Members of the Bush administration contradicted the views of the two former chairmen of the joint chiefs of staff. Cheney argued before the Armed Services panel that there was no guarantee that even in five years economic sanctions would force Saddam out of Kuwait. William H. Webster, director of the CIA, told the House Foreign Affairs Committee that "although sanctions are hurting Iraq's civilian economy, they are affecting Iraq's military only at the margins."[9] And General Colin L. Powell, the chairman of the joint chiefs of staff, reminded his interrogators that "waiting is not without cost as an option."[10]

Fifty-four members of Congress decided to test the president's war-making power in court. They signed a petition seeking an injunction (court order) to prohibit the president from taking offensive action against Iraq without the prior consent of Congress. Federal Judge Harold H. Greene ruled that such an injunction would be premature because Congress had not yet voted on the issue. Nevertheless, Judge Greene flatly rejected the White House position that Bush as commander in chief of the military forces had the legal authority to start a war. "The court is not prepared," he said, "to read out of the Constitution the clause granting to Congress, and to it alone, the authority 'to declare war.' " And there is no question, the judge added, "that an offensive entry into Iraq by several hundred thousand United States servicemen . . . could be described as a 'war' within the meaning of Article 1, Section 8, Clause 11, of the Constitution."[11]

Diplomats from the United Nations, the United States, and other countries earnestly tried to convince Saddam Hussein that he must order his troops to leave Kuwait or face drastic consequences. But the Iraqi dictator stubbornly refused to heed their advice. If hostilities began, he vowed to destroy Saudi and Kuwaiti oil fields, attack Israel, and launch the "mother of all wars" against his enemies. The coalition of countries aligned against Saddam was not deterred by his brash threats. On November 29, the UN Security Council passed resolution 678 by a 12 to 2 vote, setting January 15, 1991, as the deadline for Iraq to start withdrawing its troops from Kuwait or face the probability of military force.

The American people were badly divided on the question of whether the United States should go to war immediately if Iraq did not comply with UN demands by the January 15 deadline. A large segment of the public believed that Saddam had been given sufficient time to get his forces out of Kuwait and that his ruthless aggression against a small, virtually defenseless country must not be allowed to stand unchallenged—even if the conflict that followed resulted in the loss of American lives. Another large group felt that a military attack against Iraq should not be started until more time had been allowed for the economic sanctions to deprive that country of the oil income and foreign products it sorely needed. Antiwar demonstrations were held in many cities and towns; some protesters argued that Kuwait was not vital to the security of the United States and that no American blood should be shed in exchange for oil from the Middle East.

The frustration of many members of Congress continued to mount as the United States seemed to be moving quickly toward war without first receiving the support of the legislative branch of the government. On December 29, House Majority Leader Richard A. Gephardt said that Democratic leaders of Congress might move to cut off funding for Operation Desert Storm if President Bush ordered a military strike against Iraq without prior congressional approval. Gephardt declared that if Bush decided on his own to use force, "Congress has to reach for the only tool left, which is to cut off the funding."[12]

Bush had a serious problem in deciding whether to ask Congress to endorse a military initiative in the Middle East. While he insisted that he did not need the approval of the legislative branch before sending Americans into battle, the president knew that he would be sternly criticized for ignoring the will of Congress. On the other hand, if the legislators voted against the war issue, Bush's position would be seriously weakened and Saddam Hussein could take comfort from a damaging rift in the United States government. Since the Democrats controlled both houses of Congress—and a large number of these Democrats were opposed to an immediate war against Iraq—there was high risk in putting this matter to a vote.

The president and his White House lieutenants worked strenuously to convince legislators that Congress should pass a resolution authorizing the use of military force against Iraq. By the time the debate began on January 10, the Bush administration felt it had a majority of supporters in both houses. The American people followed this crucial debate with rapt attention. "Many who heard all or part of the televised proceedings commented on what they perceived to be its extraordinary quality," wrote one historian. "In both houses of Congress, men and women spoke carefully and thoughtfully, insisting that they had never participated in a more critical debate, on which so much depended."[13]

In the House of Representatives, Congresswoman Barbara Vucanovich, a Republican from Nevada, declared, "There can be no reward for brutal aggression. If we do nothing, and Saddam Hussein pays no price for swallowing up the country of Kuwait . . . we are as guilty as he is."[14] Among those arguing for the other side was a Vietnam veteran, Representative David E. Bonior, a Michigan Democrat. "Do we really want to go to war with a country so deeply divided on this issue?" Bonior asked.[15]

The war resolution won in the House by a vote of 250 to 183. Eighty-six Democrats voted for it; they were mainly southern conservatives and staunch supporters of Israel, a country that was extremely vulnerable to Saddam's aggression. Only three House Republicans voted against the president's position.

Both sides agreed that the count would be much closer in the Senate. Republican Minority Leader Bob Dole of Kansas, who had lost the use of his right arm in World War II, told his colleagues that "no one abhors war more than those of us who have fought in one," but he asserted that the president must be supported in his crusade to drive the Iraqis out of Kuwait.[16] The opposition in the Senate was led by Majority Leader Mitchell and Democrat Sam Nunn of Georgia, a recognized authority on national security and military affairs. "We are playing a winning hand," Nunn said. "I see no compelling reason to rush to military action."[17]

The Senate adopted the war resolution by the close vote of 52 to 47. Ten Democrats, including Albert Gore, Jr., of Tennessee, voted for the resolution. Just two Republicans, Mark Hatfield of Oregon and Charles Grassley of Iowa, voted against it.

The two houses of Congress had passed the historic resolution authorizing the president to use force against Iraq on January 12, 1991—only three days before the ultimatum to Saddam expired. Once the debate had ended, House Speaker Tom Foley, who had opposed the president's position, said, "Let us come together after this vote without recrimination. We are all Americans here—not Democrats, not Republicans."[18] When the hostilities began on January 16, members of Congress closed ranks and gave their wholehearted support to America's fighting men and women.

The war was extremely one-sided and mercifully short. It lasted only forty-three days. After less than six weeks of bombing Iraqi targets intensively, a massive ground assault was launched. After five more days of fighting, in which his overpowered troops withdrew on all fronts, Saddam agreed to a cease-fire. Only 146 Americans had been killed in combat, and another 159 died of war-related causes. An estimated 70,000 to 115,000 Iraqi troops had lost their lives, and most of Saddam's tanks and artillery had been destroyed or captured.[19] Operation Desert Storm was acclaimed a glorious success, and huge, happy crowds greeted the American warriors as they came home.

The war, however, did not end all concerns about

Iraq's military potential. Saddam remained in power, and after the cease-fire his troops brutally attacked the Kurdish people and Shiite Muslims, two minority groups who lived in Iraq. Saddam also violated some of the cease-fire conditions. He tried to hide from United Nations inspectors the components he had acquired for building atom bombs and the locations of deadly chemical and biological weapons that he still possessed. In the postwar period, questions arose about how Iraq had obtained such advanced weapons systems. Media stories began revealing that before the invasion of Kuwait American companies had shipped to Iraq various products that could be used in the manufacture of weapons, while agencies of the United States government had provided loans and credits that helped strengthen Saddam's military arsenal.

Nevertheless, some important positive results emerged from the war. From a military standpoint, the United States had demonstrated its awesome superiority. This helped Americans ease the bitter memories associated with the disastrous Vietnam War. The joining together of most Arab countries and Israel in a common cause had at least opened the door to the possibility of improved relations between Arabs and Jews. The war provided the United Nations an opportunity to take on greater importance. This was partly because the coalition it had sponsored had successfully repelled an aggressor, and also because the multinational cooperation it had achieved seemed to point the way to a possible new world order based on justice and fairness applied to the international relations of all countries.

GEORGE BUSH

THE THOMAS
APPOINTMENT

One way in which presidents can help shape national policies long after their terms of office have ended is through the appointment of federal judges, especially justices of the Supreme Court. Since federal judges serve on the bench for life, their decisions can reflect for many years the philosophy of the presidents who selected them.

While Ronald Reagan was in the White House, he had the opportunity to fill three Supreme Court vacancies, and, as expected, this conservative president nominated as justices persons who shared his conservative philosophy. One was Sandra Day O'Connor, the first woman named to the Supreme Court; another was Antonin Scalia, who had been a judge on the U.S. Court of Appeals in Washington, D.C. The Senate, which must confirm federal judicial appointments by a majority vote, cast unanimous ballots to seat both O'Connor and Scalia.

When President Reagan attempted to fill the vacancy created by the retirement of Justice Lewis F. Powell, Jr., in 1987, the Senate, which was then controlled by Democrats, hotly debated the president's appointment. The nominee was ultraconservative Robert H. Bork, a brilliant legal scholar who had been solicitor general in the Nixon administration and later was Scalia's colleague on the Court of Appeals in Washington, D.C. Bork's controversial views were widely known from the many articles he had written, and he discussed them at his Senate confirmation hearing. Bork believed that the Supreme Court "was wrong to uphold civil rights so forcefully, wrong to protect freedom of speech so broadly, and wrong to create a right to privacy," which included abortion.[1]

Civil rights activists, abortion rights supporters, and other liberal groups demanded that senators vote against Bork's appointment to the Supreme Court. After the hearing ended and the vote was taken, the Senate rejected Bork, 58 to 42, which was the largest margin of defeat ever handed to a Supreme Court nominee. This vacancy on the court later was filled by Anthony M. Kennedy, another appeals court judge, who was confirmed unanimously by the Senate.

When George Bush followed Reagan into the White House, the new Republican president wanted to add more conservatives to the Supreme Court. The first opportunity came when liberal William J. Brennan, Jr., announced in July 1988 his retirement from the high court, after thirty-four years of distinguished service. The Bush administration decided to steer clear of any nominee who might provoke strong criticism—as Bork had—that could result in his rejection by the Senate. The man nominated by the president was David H. Souter, a former New Hampshire Supreme Court judge who only weeks before had been named to the U.S. appeals court in Boston.

Souter, a quiet, studious bachelor, had not written articles or made speeches on controversial topics. At his confirmation hearing, he impressed senators with his keen knowledge of constitutional law and expressed no opinions on sensitive issues that might arouse hostility.

By a 90 to 9 vote, the Senate confirmed Souter as the 105th justice of the Supreme Court.

On June 27, 1991, Justice Thurgood Marshall, the first black member of the Supreme Court, announced his resignation. This gave Bush a second opportunity to replace a liberal justice with a conservative. Some of his advisers urged the president to nominate another black to fill this position. On July 1, Bush nominated for the Supreme Court Clarence Thomas, a forty-three-year-old black, who had practiced law for only five years of his career and had served on the federal appeals court in Washington, D.C., for a scant fifteen months. In announcing this nomination, Bush stated that Thomas was the best qualified person to sit on the high court and that race had absolutely nothing to do with his choice.

The American Bar Association (ABA), which has a committee of members who review and rate the qualifications of all judicial nominees, did not agree with the president's high assessment of Thomas. The bar association has three ratings: well qualified, qualified, and not qualified. Its committee generally has rated Supreme Court nominees as well qualified, usually unanimously so. But in August the ABA committee rated Thomas as only qualified, and not one member voted that he was well qualified.

Timothy M. Phelps and Helen Winternitz, who wrote a book on the Thomas appointment, declared that President Bush's statement that Thomas was the best qualified person for the job "was patently untrue. . . . Thousands of American lawyers had better qualifications. Thomas," they concluded, "was not even the best qualified black jurist, or black Republican jurist. Not by a long shot."[2]

Clarence Thomas's life story was a remarkable saga of one man's ceaseless, dogged determination to succeed despite economic adversity and racial prejudice.

Born on June 23, 1948, Thomas spent his first years in Pin Point, Georgia, living in a one-room wooden shack that had a dirt floor and no plumbing or electricity. His father abandoned the family when Clarence was two years old, leaving Clarence's mother the difficult job of supporting three children on a weekly wage of fifteen dollars, earned from cleaning crabs and working as a maid for a white woman. The children wore old clothes donated by the local church, and they lived on corn-flakes, crabs, and grits mixed occasionally with eggs, milk, and syrup.

At the age of seven, Clarence and his younger brother began living with their grandfather, Myers Anderson, in Savannah. Anderson was a hardworking, deeply religious Catholic, who instilled in his grandsons moral values, the importance of acquiring an education, and the often-repeated belief that self-reliance was the key to achieving success. His grandfather sternly told Clarence, "I'm not going to give you anything. What I will do is give you the opportunity to earn it."[3]

Clarence attended Catholic elementary and secondary schools, where he studied diligently and earned high grades. Then he worked his way through Holy Cross College and after graduation applied to Yale University Law School. Yale admitted Clarence in part because of a new affirmative-action policy that set up the goal that blacks and other minorities should comprise roughly 10 percent of each class. (Affirmative action is a plan or program to help remedy the effects of past racial or sexual discrimination by establishing goals and timetables to increase the participation of those classes of people who had historically been subject to discrimination.)

Like many black students in white schools, Clarence Thomas had been taunted by racial slurs and insults. But he went out of his way not to be identified by his color. At law school he avoided advanced classes on civil rights and concentrated instead on subjects such as antitrust and tax law. Moreover, although he realized that affirmative action had helped to get him into law school, he believed that it was being used excessively and that it should be based mainly on economic need, not race. To be rewarded simply because of his color contradicted the lesson that his grandfather had taught— that achievement came only from hard work and determination.

After graduation from law school, Thomas joined the staff of Missouri's Republican attorney general, John Danforth. In 1977 Danforth moved to Washington as a newly elected senator, and a short time later Thomas again went to work for Danforth, specializing in energy and environmental projects. Thomas began acquiring a reputation as a young Republican black with a bright future, and he won favor in conservative circles when, in addressing a San Francisco conference, he criticized his own sister for being on welfare and getting mad whenever the mail carrier was late with her check from the government.

Soon after Ronald Reagan became president, Thomas was appointed assistant secretary for civil rights in the Education Department. Ten months later, Reagan named him head of the Equal Employment Opportunity Commission (EEOC), the nation's chief antidiscrimination agency, where he served for eight years. As head of the EEOC, Thomas was not completely consistent in his approach to affirmative-action complaints. He generally took the position that individual acts of discrimination in hiring workers should be prosecuted vigorously, but that class-action awards based on racial statistics usually were not appropriate. In March 1990, President Bush appointed Thomas to the federal appeals court, where he wrote about twenty opinions before being nominated the next year to serve on the Supreme Court.

When Thomas appeared before the Senate Judiciary Committee at his confirmation hearing in September, he

hired as an assistant to Clarence Thomas in the Office of Civil Rights at the Department of Education. When Thomas moved to the EEOC, Hill joined his staff at this federal agency. In 1983 she abruptly left Washington, taking a job as an assistant law professor at Oral Roberts University, which was then located in Tulsa, Oklahoma. Three years later, she joined the faculty at the University of Oklahoma's law school.

When Professor Hill's sexual harassment allegations against Thomas were revealed, they were far more serious than the fact that her boss had repeatedly asked her to go on dates with him, which she consistently refused to do. She charged that in private he often talked to her about their anatomy. Hill further alleged that Thomas spoke excitedly about and recounted details of acts that he had seen in pornographic films.

Thomas was stunned and enraged by Hill's explosive charges. He denied all of them vehemently, lashing out at the public airing of what he called "a high-tech lynching for uppity blacks." He grimly stated that not even a seat on the highest court in the land was worth the pain he and his family had suffered since Hill's allegations had been disclosed. "Enough is enough," he bluntly declared.[5]

Articulate but softspoken, Hill appeared poised and calm as she repeated her charges before the fourteen-man Judiciary Committee. Republican Senators Arlen Specter of Pennsylvania, Orrin G. Hatch of Utah, and Alan Simpson of Wyoming forcefully attacked her credibility, at times suggesting that her testimony was perjured and at other times indicating that perhaps she had fantasized (imagined) the acts she accused Thomas of committing. Still, millions of television viewers believed Hill's allegations. Many women—some who had experienced sexual harassment in the workplace—sympathized with the black professor and were astonished that members of the all-male Senate panel did not seem to "get it" when a female claimed she had been sexually abused without any physical contact.

The Democratic senators who questioned Thomas appeared neither as skilled nor as energetic as the Republicans who had interrogated Hill. They failed to sustain a tough line of questioning designed to poke holes in the account given by the president's nominee. Thomas steadfastly maintained that he was innocent of Hill's charges, and his earnest, apparently sincere testimony was very impressive.

After Hill and Thomas both had appeared before the committee, it was difficult to tell which of them was lying. Friends of Hill then testified that she had privately told them of Thomas's alleged acts of sexual harrassment soon after they had occurred. Thomas then countered with witnesses who assured the committee that his conduct as an employer had always been free of even the slightest sexual abuse.

Was Thomas or Hill telling the truth? This agonizing question still had not been answered. Hill volunteered to take and passed a polygraph test. While not foolproof, this lie-detector test helped convince many people that she had testified honestly; Thomas did not submit to a test. Yet national polls showed that the public, by a large margin, believed that Thomas's testimony was truthful.

Some of the Senate Democrats who had originally planned to vote for Thomas's confirmation changed their minds after the issue of possible sexual harassment was raised. Both sides predicted that the vote would be close. On October 15, 1991, the Senate approved the appointment of Clarence Thomas to the Supreme Court by a 52 to 48 vote, the narrowest margin of approval in this century for a nominee to the nation's highest court. Eleven Democrats voted for his confirmation; two Republicans voted against it.

Far-reaching repercussions flowed from this historic event. Both Republicans and Democrats agreed that a better method should be formulated for nominating and confirming Supreme Court candidates. One suggestion was that before any appointment is announced, the president should meet with a bipartisan group of Senate leaders to carefully consider the qualifications of possible nominees. While the president still would be expected to choose someone who shared the same political philosophy, the selection process could be improved if the chief executive sought the "advice and consent" of the Senate—as the Constitution stipulates—before, as well as after, the nominee is named.

Another effect of the Thomas proceedings was the enormous momentum it provided for women to seek high political offices. Only two of the one hundred senators who voted on Thomas's confirmation were women. "This has shown the need for more women in the Senate better than the entire feminist movement has shown in the last twenty-five years," according to Katherine Spillar, national coordinator of the Fund for the Feminist Majority.

In the 1992 elections, four additional women were elected to the Senate, including Carol Moseley Braun of Illinois, the first African-American woman to serve in the Senate. The 1992 elections also sent 19 additional women to the House of Representatives, bringing the total number of women in the 435-member House to 47.

The Thomas appointment also affected passage of new civil rights legislation over which Congress and the president had haggled for nearly two years. The Civil Rights Act of 1991, which President Bush signed in November, made it easier for women and minorities to sue their employers for workplace discrimination. Also, while victims of sexual harassment previously could win only back pay in lawsuits, this new law enabled them to sue for up to $300,000 in damages.

The fight over Thomas's appointment brought scorn and disapproval to both the president and Congress.

President Bush's judgment was seriously questioned for nominating Thomas and exerting pressure on senators to approve his selection. The Senate's conduct was besmirched when the consideration of a nominee to the most important judicial office in the nation descended into an ugly, highly politicized, sleaze-centered brawl.

In a positive sense, however, the Thomas case highlighted a larger struggle in American society that has gained increasing awareness in recent years. It is "the conflict between a system dominated by traditional male values and a challenge based on female values."[7]

EPILOGUE

BALANCE OF POWERS OR PARALYZED GOVERNMENT?

When the Founding Fathers wrote the Constitution, they decided to balance the powers among the branches of the national government in order to prevent a single branch from becoming too powerful and assuming the role of a dictator. Little did they realize in 1787—before the emergence of political parties—that their balance of powers concept could lead to a partial paralysis of the national government. This deadlock in Washington, D.C., has most often occurred when there was a divided government in which the president belonged to one of the major political parties and Congress was controlled by the other.

In the first half of the twentieth century, there were not many instances of a divided government. Democratic presidents usually, but not always, served with a Congress dominated by fellow Democrats. The sweeping legislation enacted when Woodrow Wilson, Franklin D. Roosevelt, and Lyndon B. Johnson were in the White House came about largely because these Democratic presidents were supported by Democratic majorities on Capitol Hill (except for the last two years of Wilson's second term).

Republican presidents in the first half of this century also almost always enjoyed the opportunity of working with a Republican Congress. Every Republican president from 1900 through 1954 served with a Republican Senate, and the House of Representatives also was controlled by Republicans except for two years each in the administrations of William H. Taft and Herbert Hoover. In fact, beginning when the Republicans elected their first president, Abraham Lincoln in 1860, for the next ninety-four years Republican presidents could count on at least one Republican house of Congress in all but the final two years (1879–81) of Rutherford B. Hayes's administration.

The situation in which the same political party controlled both the executive and the legislative branches changed in 1954, midway through Republican President Dwight Eisenhower's first term, when the Democrats won both the Senate and the House of Representatives. This event signaled the beginning of a major new political trend. The Democrats have continued to win control of the House of Representatives in every election since 1954, and during this period they have held onto the Senate, too, except in the first six years of Ronald Reagan's administration. On the other hand, from 1969 to 1993, there were Republican presidents for twenty of the twenty-four years.

The problems caused by a divided government were apparent during the one-term administration of Republican President George Bush, who confronted a strongly Democratic Congress. When President Bush was widely criticized for not taking vigorous action to combat a serious, lingering economic recession, he blamed Congress for failing to pass economic measures he proposed, such as a reduction in some areas of government spending, a constitutional amendment to balance the budget, and a lower tax on capital gains. In describing how he felt Congress had betrayed his trust, Bush told the 1992 Republican convention, "I extended my hand to the Democratic leaders and they bit it."[1]

The Democrats in Congress replied that they had proposed various economic bills—and also important social and political measures—that President Bush squelched with the stroke of his pen. They charged that the president must be held accountable for vetoing thirty-six bills before Congress adjourned in October 1992. Except for the bill to regulate television cable rates, the lawmakers were unable to muster the two-thirds vote needed to override Bush's vetoes, so the president's opposition to the other thirty-five measures amounted to the kiss of death.

Since a divided government has failed to solve many of the country's most troublesome problems, why did the voters again and again send a Republican president to the White House and a majority of Democrats to Congress? Former Republican Congressman Vin Weber of Minnesota, who refused to run for reelection in 1992 largely because he was disillusioned with the stalemated government in the nation's capital, expressed the opinion that the American people ". . . like divided government. They don't trust either political party."[2]

Columnist Charles Krauthammer asserted that the nation could no longer afford a gridlocked government. "The Founding Fathers established a government heavily checked and balanced, paralysis being a fine bulwark against tyranny. But now it goes too far," he observed. "After all, a machine built for gridlock that spends just a few million dollars a year, as did the fledgling republic of the 1700s, is an annoyance. But a machine built for gridlock that consumes $1.4 trillion a year is a scandal."[3]

The best way to break the gridlock in the national government, according to political scientist Sidney Waldman, is to give one party control over both Congress and the presidency. "Major movement on problems has occurred when we've had united government," he declared. "In most times checks and balances is fine, but when the country faces serious problems and action is required we really need united government."[4]

In November 1992, the voters reversed the trend of sending still another divided government to Washington, D.C. They elected Democrat Bill Clinton to the presidency and a Democratic Congress. Still, there was no assurance that the president and the lawmakers would always work together harmoniously, nor that they could solve such staggering problems as reducing unemployment, curbing the huge deficit, and providing affordable health care for most Americans. But at least the executive and legislative branches of the federal government were controlled by the same party, and this, in itself, marked a new beginning.

When Clinton moved into the White House, Congress might have been expected to enact most of his legislative program because Democrats had an eighty-vote majority in the House of Representatives and a fourteen-vote majority in the Senate. However, the new president was in office only three months when Senate Republicans, voting unanimously, defeated his $16.3 billion economic stimulus plan. The tactic employed by the outnumbered Republicans to squelch this bill was to use Senate rules that permit debate to continue indefinitely unless sixty senators vote to end it. This filibuster succeeded because the Democrats were unable to muster the sixty votes needed to shut off debate.

A short time later, Congress considered a very important issue: President Clinton's budget bill that called for reducing the government deficit by about $500 billion through a combination of raising taxes and cutting government spending. Besides united Republican opposition to the bill, some liberal Democrats felt the measure was too conservative and some conservative Democrats felt it was too liberal. The president found himself caught in a trap—pinned between his party's conservative and liberal wings without a clear-cut majority of legislators who could guarantee passage of this bill that was crucial to his economic program and perhaps to the success of his presidency.

When the budget bill reached the House floor in May 1993, it passed by only six votes. Thirty-eight Democrats voted against it, and a switch of only three votes would have killed it. The margin of victory in the Senate was razor thin; Vice President Al Gore, the presiding officer of the Senate, had to cast the tie-breaking vote that saved the measure from defeat. Then a conference committee consisting of members from both houses of Congress had to iron out the differences between the House and Senate versions of this bill.

The final vote on this budget bill—the first major test of the Clinton administration—occurred in August 1993. By a vote of 218 to 216, the House of Representatives approved it; 41 Democrats joined 175 Republicans in opposing it. In the Senate, once again the vote was tied until Vice President Gore cast his ballot favoring the measure. If one more legislator in either house of Congress had voted against the bill, it would not have passed.

President Clinton eked out a narrow victory on the budget bill by the slimmest of margins. The closeness of the vote in both houses of Congress indicated that the struggle between the executive and legislative branches of the federal government, which began during George Washington's administration, still continues more than two centuries after the birth of the nation.

NOTES

CHAPTER I

1. George Fort Milton, *The Use of Presidential Power, 1789–1943* (Boston: Little, Brown, 1944), p. 37.

2. Hugh G. Gallagher, *Advise and Obstruct: The Role of the United States Senate in Foreign Policy Decisions* (New York: Delacorte, 1969), p. 50.

3. Walter LaFeber, *The American Age: United States Foreign Policy at Home and Abroad Since 1750* (New York: Norton, 1989), p. 46.

4. Edmund Lindop, *By a Single Vote! One-Vote Decisions That Changed American History* (Harrisburg, Pa.: Stackpole, 1987), p. 20.

5. Ernest Sutherland Bates, *The Story of Congress, 1789–1935* (New York: Harper, 1936), p. 29.

6. Thomas A. Bailey, *A Diplomatic History of the American People* (New York: Crofts, 1946), p. 67.

7. Gallagher, *Advise and Obstruct*, p. 73.

8. Bates, *Story of Congress*, p. 34.

CHAPTER II

1. Page Smith, *The Nation Comes of Age* (New York: McGraw-Hill, 1981), p. 60.

2. Alvin M. Josephy, Jr., *On the Hill: A History of the American Congress* (New York: Simon and Schuster, 1979), p. 175.

3. Ibid.

4. *The American Heritage Pictorial History of the Presidents of the United States* (New York: American Heritage, 1968), vol. 1, p. 208.

5. William A. DeGregorio, *The Complete Book of U.S. Presidents* (New York: Dembner, 1984), p. 116.

6. Josephy, *On the Hill*, p. 178.

CHAPTER III

1. Ernest Sutherland Bates, *The Story of Congress, 1789–1935* (New York: Harper, 1936), p. 218.

2. Richard M. Pious, *The American Presidency* (New York: Basic Books, 1979), p. 56.

3. James M. McPherson, *Abraham Lincoln and the Second American Revolution* (New York: Oxford University Press, 1990), p. 29.

4. Ibid., p. 57.

5. Arthur M. Schlesinger, Jr., *The Imperial Presidency* (Boston: Houghton Mifflin, 1973), p. 59.

6. J. E. Randall, *The Civil War and Reconstruction* (Lexington, Mass: D. C. Heath, 1937), p. 361.

7. Schlesinger, *Imperial Presidency*, p. 59.

8. Pious, *American Presidency*, p. 58.

9. James MacGregor Burns, *The Deadlock of Democracy: Four-Party Politics in America* (Englewood Cliffs, N.J.: Prentice-Hall, 1963), p. 72.

10. Randall, *Civil War*, p. 605.

11. Alvin M. Josephy, Jr., *On the Hill: A History of the American Congress* (New York: Simon and Schuster, 1979), pp. 220–21.

12. Burns, *Deadlock*, p. 73.

CHAPTER IV

1. Alvin M. Josephy, Jr., *On the Hill: A History of the American Congress* (New York: Simon and Schuster, 1979), p. 223.

2. James T. Currie, *The United States House of Representatives* (Malabar, Fla.: Krieger, 1988), p. 43.

3. Richard A. Baker, *The Senate of the United States: A Bicentennial History* (Malabar, Fla.: Krieger, 1988), p. 59.

4. Irving Brant, *Impeachment: Trials and Errors* (New York: Knopf, 1972), p. 136.

5. John F. Kennedy, *Profiles in Courage* (New York: Harper, 1955), p. 148.

CHAPTER V

1. Paul F. Boller, Jr., *Congressional Anecdotes* (New York: Oxford University Press, 1991), p. 267.

2. Arthur S. Link, *American Epoch: A History of the United States Since 1890* (New York: Knopf, 1959), p. 220.

3. Philip C. Dolce and George H. Skau, eds., *Power and the Presidency* (New York: Scribner's, 1976), p. 82.

4. Walter LaFeber, *The American Age: United States Foreign Policy at Home and Abroad Since 1750* (New York: Norton, 1989), pp. 307–8.

5. Boller, *Congressional Anecdotes*, pp. 289–90.

6. Gene Smith, *When the Cheering Stopped: The Last Years of Woodrow Wilson* (New York: Morrow, 1964), p. 65.

CHAPTER VI

1. Edmund Lindop, *The Turbulent Thirties* (New York: Franklin Watts, 1970), p. 23.
2. Edward S. Corwin, *The President: Office and Powers, 1787–1957* (New York: New York University Press, 1957), p. 290.
3. William Manchester, *The Glory and the Dream: A Narrative History of America, 1932–1972* (Boston: Little, Brown, 1973), vol. 1, p. 183.
4. Ibid., p. 184.

CHAPTER VII

1. William E. Leuchtenburg, *In the Shadow of FDR: From Harry Truman to Ronald Reagan* (Ithaca, N.Y.: Cornell University Press, 1983), p. 7.
2. Ibid, p. 9.
3. Michael Barone, *Our Country: The Shaping of America from Roosevelt to Reagan* (New York: Free Press, 1990), p. 187.

CHAPTER VIII

1. Stephen E. Ambrose, *Eisenhower, the President* (New York: Simon and Schuster, 1984), p. 68.
2. William Manchester, *The Glory and the Dream: A Narrative History of America, 1932–1972* (Boston: Little, Brown, 1973), vol. 1, p. 823.
3. Dwight D. Eisenhower, *Mandate for Change, 1953–1956* (New York: Doubleday, 1963), p. 280.
4. Robert J. Donovan, *Eisenhower, the Inside Story* (New York: Harper, 1956), p. 239.
5. Manchester, *Glory and the Dream*, p. 825.
6. Richard A. Baker, *The Senate of the United*

States: A Bicentennial History (Malabar, Fla.: Krieger, 1988), p. 96.

CHAPTER IX

1. *Los Angeles Times*, May 19, 1991, p. M-1.

2. Thomas P. O'Neill and William Novak, *Man of the House: The Life and Political Memoirs of Speaker Tip O'Neill* (New York: Random House, 1987), p. 165.

3. *New York Times, The Kennedy Years* (New York: Viking, 1964), p. 280.

4. James MacGregor Burns, *The Crosswinds of Freedom* (New York: Knopf, 1989), p. 369.

5. Richard B. Morris and Jeffrey B. Morris, *Great Presidential Decisions: State Papers That Changed the Course of History from Washington to Reagan* (New York: Richardson, Steirman and Black, 1988), p. 445.

6. Stephen K. Bailey, *The New Congress* (New York: St. Martin's, 1966), p. 75.

7. Marcus Cunliffe, *American Presidents and the Presidency* (New York: McGraw-Hill, 1976), p. 332.

CHAPTER X

1. Walter LaFeber, *The American Age: United States Foreign Policy at Home and Abroad Since 1750* (New York: Norton, 1989), p. 522.

2. Ibid.

3. Milton Meltzer, *Ain't Gonna Study War No More* (New York: Harper and Row, 1985), p. 234.

4. Richard M. Pious, *The American Presidency* (New York: Basic Books, 1979), p. 399.

5. Ibid.

6. Michael Barone, *Our Country: The Shaping of*

America from Roosevelt to Reagan (New York: Free Press, 1990), p. 398.

7. Jules Witcover, *85 Days: The Last Campaign of Robert Kennedy* (New York: Morrow, 1988), p. 264.

8. Harvey C. Mansfield, ed., *Congress against the President* (Washington, D.C.: Academy of Political Science, 1975), p. 170.

9. Eugene H. Roseboom and Alfred E. Eckles Jr., *A History of Presidential Elections from George Washington to Jimmy Carter* (New York: Macmillan, 1979), p. 300.

10. *Powers of Congress* (Washington, D.C.: Congressional Quarterly, 1982), p. 118.

11. Ibid.

CHAPTER XI

1. Bob Woodward and Carl Bernstein, *The Final Days* (New York: Simon and Schuster, 1976), p. 458.

2. *Watergate: Chronology of a Crisis* (Washington, D.C.: Congressional Quarterly, 1974), p. 458.

3. Ibid.

4. James MacGregor Burns, *The Crosswinds of Freedom* (New York: Knopf, 1989), p. 503.

5. Richard M. Pious, *The American Presidency* (New York: Basic Books, 1979), p. 76.

6. Alvin M. Josephy, Jr., *On the Hill: A History of the American Congress* (New York: Simon and Schuster, 1979), pp. 370–71.

7. *Powers of Congress* (Washington, D.C.: Congressional Quarterly, 1982), p. 224.

8. Burns, *Crosswinds*, p. 506.

9. William A. DeGregorio, *The Complete Book of Presidents* (New York: Dembner, 1984), p. 612.

10. Thomas P. O'Neill and William Novak, *Man of the House: The Life and Political Memoirs of*

Speaker Tip O'Neill (New York: Random House, 1987), p. 271.

CHAPTER XII

1. Gary Wills, *Reagan's America: Innocents at Home* (Garden City, N.Y.: Doubleday, 1987), p. 330.

2. Michael Barone, *Our Country: The Shaping of America from Roosevelt to Reagan* (New York: Free Press, 1990), p. 570.

3. Jimmy Carter, *Keeping Faith: Memoirs of a President* (New York: Bantam, 1982), p. 155.

4. Ibid.

5. Richard B. Morris and Jeffrey B. Morris, *Great Presidential Decisions: State Papers That Changed the Course of History from Washington to Reagan* (New York: Richardson, Steirman and Black, 1988), p. 504.

6. Ibid.

CHAPTER XIII

1. Stephen R. Graubard, *Mr. Bush's War: Adventures in the Politics of Illusion* (New York: Hill and Wang, 1992), p. 50.

2. *The Iran-Contra Puzzle* (Washington, D.C.: Congressional Quarterly, 1987), p. A-10.

3. Lou Cannon, *President Reagan: The Role of a Lifetime* (New York: Simon and Schuster, 1991), p. 590.

4. Richard B. Morris and Jeffrey B. Morris, *Great Presidential Decisions: State Papers That Changed the Course of History from Washington to Reagan* (New York: Richardson, Steirman and Black, 1988), p. 521.

5. William S. Cohen and George J. Mitchell, *Men of Zeal: A Candid Inside Story of the Iran-Contra Hearings* (New York: Viking, 1988), p. 12.

6. *Joint Hearings of the Iran-Contra Investigation: Testimony of John M. Poindexter* (Washington, D.C.: Government Printing Office, 1988), p. 37.

7. Cohen and Mitchell, *Men of Zeal*, pp. 310–11.

CHAPTER XIV

1. Judith Miller and Laurie Mylorie, *Saddam Hussein and the Crisis in the Gulf* (New York: Times Books/Random House, 1990), p. 192.

2. Jean Edward Smith, *George Bush's War* (New York: Holt, 1992), p. 100.

3. Ibid., pp. 180–81.

4. *Time*, Jan. 14, 1991, p. 13.

5. *Time, Dec. 17, 1990, p. 33.*

6. *Los Angeles Times*, Jan. 10, 1991, p. A-1.

7. *Los Angeles Times*, Dec. 5, 1990, p. A-10.

8. *Los Angeles Times*, Dec. 6, 1990, p. A-8.

9. Ibid.

10. Ibid.

11. *Los Angeles Times*, Dec. 14, 1990, p. A-22.

12. *Los Angeles Times*, Dec. 30, 1990, p. A-1.

13. Stephen R. Graubard, *Mr. Bush's War: Adventures in the Politics of Illusion* (New York: Hill and Wang, 1992), p. 121.

14. *Congressional Record*, 102nd Congress, 1st Session, vol. 137, Jan. 12, 1991, p. H-169.

15. *Los Angeles Times*, Jan. 13, 1991, p. A-7.

16. Ibid.

17. *Congressional Record*, 102nd Congress, 1st Session, vol. 137, Jan. 12, 1991, p. S-367.

18. *U.S. News and World Report, Triumph without Victory: The Unreported History of the Persian Gulf War* (New York: Times Books/Random House, 1992), p. 207.

19. *Newsweek*, Jan. 20, 1992, p. 18.

CHAPTER XV

1. David G. Savage, *Turning Right: The Making of the Rehnquist Supreme Court* (New York: Wiley, 1992), p. 146.

2. Timothy M. Phelps and Helen Winternitz, *Capitol Games: Clarence Thomas, Anita Hill, and the Story of a Supreme Court Nomination* (New York: Hyperion, 1992), p. 16.

3. *Newsweek*, Sept. 16, 1991, p. 23.

4. *Los Angeles Times*, Sept. 28, 1991, p. A-24.

5. *Los Angeles Times*, Oct. 12, 1991, p. A-1.

6. *Los Angeles Times*, Oct. 16, 1991, p. A-6.

7. Phelps and Winternitz, *Capitol Games*, p. 329.

EPILOGUE

1. *Los Angeles Times*, Aug. 29, 1992, p. A-5.

2. *Time*, June 8, 1992, p. 65.

3. *Time*, Dec. 9, 1991, p. 92.

4. *USA Today*, Apr. 27, 1992, p. 7-A.

FOR FURTHER READING

Ambrose, Stephen E. *Eisenhower, the President.* New York: Simon and Schuster, 1984.

Arnson, Cynthia J. *Crossroads: Congress, the Reagan Administration, and Central America.* New York: Pantheon, 1989.

Baker, Richard A. *The Senate of the United States: A Bicentennial History.* Malabar, Fla.: Krieger, 1988.

Barone, Michael. *Our Country: The Shaping of America from Roosevelt to Reagan.* New York: Free Press, 1990.

Boller, Paul F., Jr. *Congressional Anecdotes.* New York: Oxford University Press, 1991.

Brant, Irving. *Impeachment: Trials and Errors.* New York: Knopf, 1972.

Burns, James MacGregor. *The Crosswinds of Freedom.* New York: Knopf, 1989.

Cannon, Lou. *President Reagan: The Role of a Lifetime.* New York: Simon and Schuster, 1991.

Carter, Jimmy. *Keeping Faith: Memoirs of a President.* New York: Bantam, 1982.

Cohen, William S., and George J. Mitchell. *Men of Zeal:*

A Candid Inside Story of the Iran-Contra Hearings. New York: Viking, 1988.

Cronin, Thomas E. *The State of the Presidency.* Boston: Little, Brown, 1980.

Currie, James T. *The United States House of Representatives.* Malabar, Fla.: Krieger, 1988.

DeGregorio, William A. *The Complete Book of U.S. Presidents.* New York: Dembner, 1984.

Dolce, Philip C., and George H. Skau, eds. *Power and the Presidency.* New York: Scribner's, 1976.

Donovan, Robert J. *Tumultuous Years: The Presidency of Harry S. Truman, 1949–1953.* New York: Norton, 1982.

Eagleton, Thomas F. *War and Presidential Power: A Chronicle of Congressional Surrender.* New York: Liveright, 1974.

Fisher, Louis. *The Politics of Shared Power: Congress and the Executive.* Washington, D.C.: Congressional Quarterly, 1987.

Franck, Thomas, and Edward Weisband. *Foreign Policy by Congress.* New York: Oxford University Press, 1979.

Fribourg, Marjorie G. *The U.S. Congress: Men Who Steered Its Course, 1787–1867.* Philadelphia: Macrae Smith, 1972.

Gallagher, Hugh G. *Advise and Obstruct: The Role of the United States Senate in Foreign Policy Decisions.* New York: Delacorte, 1969.

Graubard, Stephen R. *Mr. Bush's War: Adventures in the Politics of Illusion.* New York: Hill and Wang, 1992.

The Iran-Contra Puzzle. Washington, D.C.: Congressional Quarterly, 1987.

Josephy, Alvin M., Jr. *On the Hill: A History of the American Congress.* New York: Simon and Schuster, 1979.

King, Anthony, ed. *Both Ends of the Avenue: The Presi-*

dency, the Executive Branch, and Congress in the 1980s. Washington, D.C.: American Enterprise Institute for Public Policy Research, 1983.

LaFeber, Walter. *The American Age: United States Foreign Policy at Home and Abroad Since 1750*. New York: Norton, 1989.

Leuchtenburg, William E. *In the Shadow of FDR: From Harry Truman to Ronald Reagan*. Ithaca, N.Y.: Cornell University Press, 1983.

Lindop, Edmund. *Presidents by Accident*. New York: Franklin Watts, 1991.

McCullough, David. *Truman*. New York: Simon and Schuster, 1992.

McPherson, James M. *Abraham Lincoln and the Second American Revolution*. New York: Oxford University Press, 1990.

Manchester, William. *The Glory and the Dream: A Narrative History of America, 1932–1972*. Boston: Little, Brown, 1973.

Meltzer, Milton. *Ain't Gonna Study War No More*. New York: Harper and Row, 1985.

Morris, Richard B., and Jeffrey B. Morris. *Great Presidential Decisions: State Papers That Changed the Course of History from Washington to Reagan*. New York: Richardson, Steirman and Black, 1988.

O'Neill, Thomas P., and William Novak. *Man of the House: The Life and Political Memoirs of Speaker Tip O'Neill*. New York: Random House, 1987.

Phelps, Timothy M., and Helen Winternitz. *Capitol Games: Clarence Thomas, Anita Hill, and the Story of a Supreme Court Nomination*. New York: Hyperion, 1992.

Pious, Richard M. *The American Presidency*. New York: Basic Books, 1979.

Powers of Congress. Washington, D.C.: Congressional Quarterly, 1982.

Schlesinger, Arthur M., Jr. *The Imperial Presidency.* Boston: Houghton Mifflin, 1973.

Smith, Jean Edward. *George Bush's War.* New York: Times Books/Random House, 1992.

Smith, Page. *The Nation Comes of Age.* New York: McGraw-Hill, 1981.

Watergate: Chronology of a Crisis. Washington, D.C.: Congressional Quarterly, 1974.

Wills, Gary. *Reagan's America: Innocents at Home.* Garden City, N.Y.: Doubleday, 1987.

Woodward, Bob, and Carl Bernstein. *All the President's Men.* New York: Simon and Schuster, 1974.

————. *The Final Days.* New York: Simon and Schuster, 1976.

INDEX